HOME OFFICE

Annual Statistics of Scientific Procedures on Living Animals

GREAT BRITAIN
2012

Presented to Parliament pursuant to section 21(7) of
the Animals (Scientific Procedures) Act 1986

Ordered by the House of Commons
to be printed 16 July 2013

HC 549   LONDON: The Stationery Office   £10.75

3301234747

ISBN: 9780102986518

Printed in the UK by The Stationery Office Limited
on behalf of the Controller of Her Majesty's Stationery Office

ID 2573951 07/13

Printed on paper containing 75% recycled fibre content minimum.

Contents

Note: The 'Supplementary Tables' and 'Time Series Tables' and the 'User Guide to Home Office Statistics of Scientific Procedures on Living Animals' can be found on the website at: https://www.gov.uk/government/publications/statistics-of-scientific-procedures-on-living-animals-great-britain-2012.

This page is intentionally blank

Introductory Notes

The statistics in this publication relate to scientific procedures performed using living animals subject to the provisions of the Animals (Scientific Procedures) Act 1986, during the year 2012. The purpose of the publication is to meet the requirements of the Animals (Scientific Procedures) Act 1986 section 21(7) "The Secretary of State shall in each year publish and lay before Parliament such information as he considers appropriate with respect to the use of protected animals in the previous year for experimental or other scientific purposes". The system of control under the 1986 Act is explained in detail in Appendix A.

Confidentiality and data quality

Detailed information on the work of individual project licence holders is not readily identifiable in this publication. Where a further breakdown of the 'other' species categories is not given in the commentary this is to safeguard the confidentiality of the establishment and the licence holder. The data are subject to revision in accordance with the Home Office's revisions policy. For more information, please see the User Guide to Home Office Statistics of Scientific Procedures on Living Animals, hereafter referred to as the User Guide.

Symbols used in tables

..	not available
-	nil
N/A	not applicable
r	revised

Acknowledgements

This publication and the accompanying web tables have been prepared by staff in the Home Office Statistics unit of the Home Office Science Group. We are grateful for the contribution of licensees who provided the returns on which this report is based. We are also grateful for the support of colleagues in the Policing Data Collection Section for data input; the Animals in Science Regulation Unit for their assistance with the collection, processing and quality assurance processes involved in preparing this report; and colleagues in the Communications Development Section who assisted in preparing the report for publication.

Uses of the statistics

The statistics are used to inform the general public, by the Government for policy decisions, for resource allocation, to inform private sector commercial choices, to support third sector activity and to facilitate academic research. For more detailed information, please refer to the User Guide.

Further information available

This publication is available online at: https://www.gov.uk/government/publications/statistics-of-scientific-procedures-on-living-animals-great-britain-2012. The website also includes:

- the 'User Guide to Home Office Statistics of Scientific Procedures on Living Animals' (a useful online reference guide which includes explanatory notes on the issues and classifications which are key to the production and presentation of the statistics);

- the 'Supplementary Tables' and the 'Time Series Tables'.

The dates of forthcoming publications are pre-announced and listed on the UK National Statistics Publication Hub: http://www.statistics.gov.uk/hub/index.html.

Home Office Responsible Statistician

David Blunt, Chief Statistician and Head of Profession for Statistics

Information on how Home Office Statistics outputs are published independently as part of the Code of Practice for Official Statistics is available at https://www.gov.uk/government/organisations/home-office/about/statistics.

Enquiries

If you have any enquiries about this publication, please email asp.statistics@homeoffice.gsi.gov.uk or write to:

Home Office Statistics, 5th Floor, Peel Building, 2 Marsham Street, London, SW1P 4DF.

> **Definition** – for the compilation of these statistics the number of procedures reported generally corresponds to the number of animals. A procedure, as regulated by law, is an experiment (or other scientific procedure) conducted on a living animal which has the effect of causing that animal pain, suffering, distress or lasting harm. Please see the User Guide for the legal definition. Where an animal that has recovered fully from a completed procedure is used again for a further procedure it is counted as a separate procedure.
>
> **Presentation** – the figures given refer to the numbers of procedures that were started in 2012 (rather than the numbers of animals), compared with 2011, unless indicated otherwise. Some figures have been rounded depending on the size of the figures in a particular section of commentary.

Summary

1. In 2012, 4.11 million scientific procedures were started in Great Britain, an increase of eight per cent (+317,200 procedures) compared with 2011. The rise was mainly attributable to a 22 per cent (+363,100) increase in the breeding of genetically modified (GM) animals[1] and harmful mutants (HM)[2], mainly mice, to 1.98 million procedures, nearly half (48%) of the total number of procedures performed. Excluding the breeding of GM and HM animals, the total number of procedures decreased by two per cent (-46,000) to 2.13 million procedures.

2. For the first time, the number of procedures involving GM animals (1.91 million) was greater than the number performed on normal animals (1.68 million).

3. There were increases in 2012 in the numbers of procedures for the following species: mice (+379,058 or +14%); sheep (+5,157 or +14%); goats (+1,462 or +746%), up from 196; guinea pigs (+1,203 or +10%); and non-human primates (+545 or +22%). There were falls for the following species: fish (-63,073 or -11%); amphibians (-2,218 or -14%); rabbits (-1,595 or -10%); and pigs (-961 or -22%).

4. The numbers of procedures for safety testing (toxicology[3]) decreased by six per cent (-22,100) to 377,000, with a greater proportion to 2011 carried out to meet at least one legislative/regulatory requirement (94% compared with 84%).

5. The number of non-toxicology procedures increased by ten per cent (+339,200) to 3.73 million and included rises for the following fields of research: nutrition (79,300 or +425%); anatomy[4] (73,200 or +20%); cancer research (69,000 or +16%); genetics[5] (+46,000 or +13%); ecology[6] (+33,100 or +85%); and biochemistry[7] (+15,800 or +54%). There were falls in the fields of physiology[8] (-173,600 or -29%); pharmaceutical research and development (-24,600 or -11%); and pharmacology[9] (-10,100 or -14%).

[1] Genetically modified animals are animals whose genetic characteristics have been altered using genetic engineering, which produces a new trait in an animal or a biological substance, such as a protein or hormone. For a more detailed description, please see the User Guide.

[2] Harmful mutants are animals possessing one or more genes that have undergone mutation, which involves a change in their genetic structure. For a more detailed description, please see the User Guide.

[3] For the purposes of these statistics, toxicology means the safety evaluation of the effects of substances on man, animals or the environment, mainly medical treatments.

[4] The study of a physical structure of an organism.

[5] The study of genes, heredity, and variation in living organisms.

[6] The study of interactions among organisms and their environment.

[7] The study of chemical processes within, and relating to, living organisms.

[8] The study of the functions of the individual structures and systems within an organism.

[9] The study of drugs.

6. There were 1.49 million more procedures (+57%) than in 2001 (which had the lowest figure since 1955), primarily due to increases in the use of breeding to produce GM or HM animals (+1.20 million or +155%) and fundamental biological research[10] (+525,400 or +67%), although there was also a notable decrease in procedures for applied studies[11] in human medicine or dentistry (-194,200 or -28%). Mice primarily accounted for the rises for both GM and HM animals (+1.04 million) and fundamental biological research (+412,600). Excluding GM or HM breeding, the total number of procedures was higher than in 2001 (+284,500 or +15%).

(Source: Tables 1, 3, 6, 9, 10, 19; and online Time Series Tables 20, 26)

---

[10] Fundamental biological research is carried out with the primary intention of increasing knowledge of the structure, function and malfunction of man and other animals, or plants. Please see the User Guide for more details.

[11] Consists of research into, development of and quality control of products or devices. See User Guide for more information.

Commentary

Procedures started in 2012

(Tables 1, 1a; and online Time Series Tables 20, 26)

There were 4.11 million scientific procedures started in 2012, an increase of 317,200 (+8%) compared with 2011. The rise was mainly attributable to an increase of 363,100 (+22%) in the breeding of genetically modified (GM) animals[12] and harmful mutants (HM)[13], mainly mice, to 1.98 million procedures, nearly half (48%) of the total number of procedures performed. Excluding the breeding of GM and HM animals, the total number of procedures decreased by 46,000 (-2%) to 2.13 million procedures. There were 4.03 million animals used for the first time in procedures started in 2012, an increase of 322,700 (+9%), reflecting the increase in the numbers of procedures started.

Figure 1 shows that the number of experiments increased considerably between 1945 and 1971, rising from 1.18 million to 5.61 million (+4.43 million or +377%), and from that period on to 1986 the number decreased to 3.11 million (-2.50 million or -45%). The implementation of the Animals (Scientific Procedures) Act 1986 changed the methodology of the collection from experiments to procedures[14] and in 1987 data were collected based on both measures, the combined figure being 3.63 million experiments/procedures.

From 1988 onwards data for procedures alone were collected and in the following years the number decreased to 2.62 million in 2001 (-882,600 or -25%), mainly due to a reduction in the use of rats, mice, all other rodents[15], rabbits, and birds (although there was an increase in the number of procedures performed on fish). Since then, the number of procedures has risen to 4.11 million in 2012 (+1.49 million or +57%), primarily due to increases in breeding to produce GM or HM animals (+1.20 million

---

[12] Genetically modified animals are animals whose genetic characteristics have been altered using genetic engineering, which produces a new trait in an animal or a biological substance, such as a protein or hormone. For a more detailed description, please see the User Guide.

[13] Harmful mutants are animals possessing one or more genes that have undergone mutation, which involves a change in their genetic structure. For a more detailed description, please see the User Guide.

[14] The Cruelty to Animals Act 1876 covered all animals which were used in experiments i.e. a procedure of unknown outcome. The Animals (Scientific Procedures) Act 1986 has a broader definition as it includes all scientific procedures which may cause pain, suffering, distress or lasting harm. Therefore, the change in methodology accounted for the increase in figures from 1987 onwards.

[15] Includes guinea pigs, hamsters, gerbils, and other rodent species.

or +155%) and fundamental biological research[16] (+525,400 or +67%), with mice mainly accounting for the rises.

The overall level of scientific procedures is determined by a number of factors, including the economic climate and global trends in scientific endeavour. In recent years, while many types of research have declined or even ended, the advent of modern scientific techniques has opened up new research areas, with genetically modified animals, mainly mice, often being required to support these areas.

Figure 1: Experiments or procedures commenced each year, 1945–2012

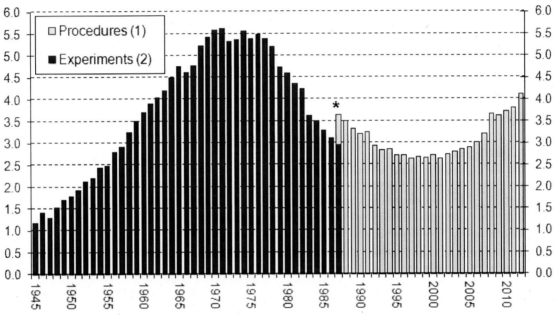

Millions of procedures

(1) Scientific Procedures under the 1986 Act
(2) Experiments under the 1876 Act
* The 1987 total includes experiments under the 1876 Act as well as procedures under the 1986 Act.

Primary purpose
(Tables 1 and 1a)

Figure 2 below compares breeding to produce GM and HM animals with other primary purposes. It shows that breeding to produce GM or HM animals increased from 312,700 in 1995 to 1.98 million in 2012 (+1.67 million or 534%). Following on from that trend, the proportion of the total number of procedures accounted for by breeding to produce GM or HM animals rose from 12 per cent in 1995 to 48 per cent in 2012, nearly half of the total number of procedures performed.

The number of procedures undertaken for other primary purposes generally declined between 1995 to 2005, decreasing from 2.40 million to 1.87 million (-528,000 or -22%). The figure then rose to 2.27 million in 2008, fell to 2.09 million the following year and has remained relatively stable since with the figure being 2.13 million in 2012.

The most common primary purposes throughout the period, other than breeding to produce GM or HM

---

[16] Fundamental biological research is carried out with the primary intention of increasing knowledge of the structure, function and malfunction of man and other animals, or plants. Please see the User Guide for more details.

animals, were fundamental biological research and applied studies[17] in human medicine or dentistry.

Figure 2: Comparison of breeding to produce GM and HM animals with other primary purposes, 1995–2012

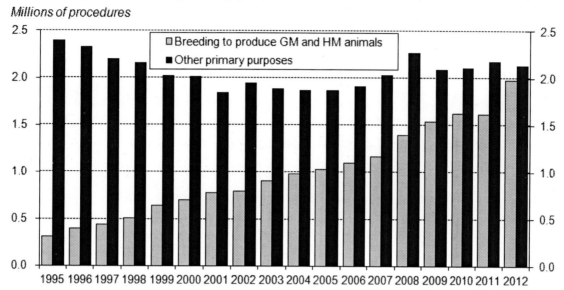

Increases

There were increases in the numbers of procedures between 2011 and 2012 for the following primary purposes:

- breeding of GM or HM animals (+363,000 or +22%);
- applied studies in human medicine or dentistry (+12,900 or +3%);
- direct diagnosis[18] (+3,600 or +8%).

Decreases

There were decreases in the numbers of procedures between 2011 and 2012 for the following primary purposes:

- fundamental biological research (-34,800 or -3%);
- protection of man, animals or environment[19] (-17,000 or -15%);
- applied studies in veterinary medicine (-10,600 or -6%).

[17] Consists of research into, development of and quality control of products or devices. See User Guide for more information.
[18] Direct diagnosis is the investigation of disease including investigating suspected poisoning. Please see the User Guide for more information.
[19] Refers to using toxicological or other safety or environmental evaluation to protect man, animals or the environment.

Species used
(Tables 1, 1a and online Time Series Table 20)

Figure 3 below shows that:

- Mice were the most commonly used species accounting for around three-quarters of procedures (74%).

- Fish (12%), rats (7%) and birds[20] (4%) were the next most frequently used species. Domestic fowl accounted for 89 per cent of all procedures using birds.

- Other mammals[21] accounted for two per cent of all procedures, of which dogs, cats and non-human primates combined were used in 0.2 per cent of all procedures, with a combined total of 8,100.

- Other rodents[22] and reptiles/amphibians accounted for 0.4 per cent and 0.3 per cent of procedures respectively.

Figure 3: Procedures by species of animal, 2012

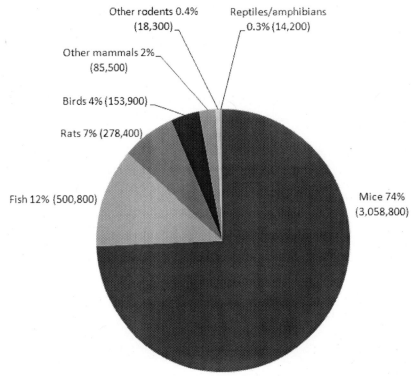

<u>Increases</u>

There were higher numbers of procedures using some species in 2012, as follows:

- mice (+379,058 or +14 %);

- sheep (+5,157 or +14%);

---

[20] Includes domestic fowl (Gallus domesticus), turkeys, all species of quail, and other bird species. The species are grouped together for the purposes of the pie chart but data are collected and published on them separately.
[21] Includes rabbits, cats, dogs, ferrets, other carnivores, horses and other equids, pigs, goats, sheep, cattle, deer, marmosets/tamarins, macaques and other mammal species. The species are grouped together for the purposes of the pie chart but data are collected and published on them separately.
[22] Includes guinea pigs, hamsters, gerbils, and other rodent species. The species are grouped together for the purposes of the pie chart but data are collected and published on them separately.

- goats (+1,462 or +746%), up from 196;

- guinea pigs (+1,203 or 10%);

- non-human primates[23] (+545 or +22%), with New World monkeys[24] (-68 or -19%) and Old World monkeys[25] (+613 or +29%).

Decreases

There were lower numbers of procedures using other species in 2012, as follows:

- fish (-63,073 or -11%);

- amphibians (-2,218 or -14%);

- rabbits (-1,595 or -10%);

- pigs (-961 or -22%).

Use of mice, rats, and fish

Figure 4 below details the numbers of procedures on the most common species used (mice, rats and fish). The chart shows that there has been a decline in the use of rats, falling from 694,400 in 1995 to 271,500 in 2011 (-61% or -422,800) but the figure increased slightly to 278,400 in 2012. The number of procedures using mice, the most frequently used species of the three throughout the series, rose from 1.45 million in 1995 to 2.63 million in 2009 (+81% or +1.17 million). The figure remained relatively stable for a couple of years then rose to 3.06 million in 2012. The overall trend for fish has seen their numbers gradually grow from 131,100 to 500,800 over the same period (+282% or 369,700), with fish being more commonly used than rats from 2008 onwards. The proportion of total procedures accounted for by mice, rats and fish has steadily increased from 84 per cent in 1995 to 93 per cent in 2012.

---

[23] The definition for non-human primates includes prosimians, New World monkeys, Old World monkeys, and apes. However, in recent years only procedures on New World monkeys and Old World monkeys have been undertaken.
[24] The definition for New World (i.e. the Americas and Oceania) monkeys includes marmosets/tarmarins; squirrel, owl, and spider monkeys; and other New World monkeys. However, in recent years, including both 2011 and 2012, only marmosets have been used in procedures.
[25] The definition for Old World (i.e. Europe, Asia, and Africa) monkeys includes macaques, baboons, and other Old World monkeys. However, in recent years, including both 2011 and 2012, only macaques have been used in procedures.

Figure 4: Procedures using mice, rats and fish 1995-2012

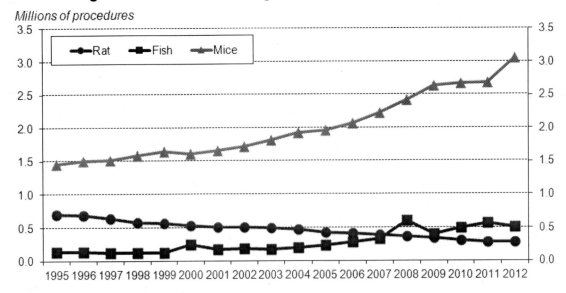

Millions of procedures

Primate use

Figure 5 below shows the change in the numbers of procedures using Old World and New World monkeys from 1995 to 2012. The use of the former was more common than that of the latter throughout the series, apart from in 1997. From that year until 2008 the overall trend was that the number of procedures on Old World monkeys increased (+56% or +1,510), as they have been required for more regulatory testing to meet legal requirements, whilst for New World monkeys (specifically marmosets) the number of procedures decreased (-82% or -1,633), as changing patterns of research have led to a decline in their use. Between 2008 and 2011 there was a fall in the use of Old World monkeys but the numbers again increased in 2012 to 2,737; however, the figure was still lower than the majority of years in the previous decade. There was a rise in the use of New World monkeys between 2008 and 2010, decreasing from then on to 283 in 2012, its lowest ever figure in the series.

Figure 5: Procedures using New World and Old World monkeys, 1995–2012

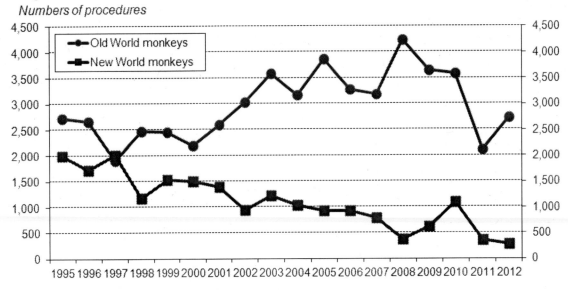

Numbers of procedures

Comparing the changes between just 2011 and 2012:

- The number of procedures using New World monkeys (i.e. marmosets/tamarins only in this comparison) fell by 68 (-19%) to 283, and the number of animals used also decreased by 12 to 232.

- The number of procedures using Old World monkeys (i.e. macaques only in this comparison) rose by 613 (+29%) to 2,737, and the number of animals used also increased by 739 to 1,954.

- Some primates were used more than once since some of the procedures they were involved in had only a minimal effect.

- Overall, the total number of procedures using non-human primates increased by 545 (+22%) to 3,020 and the number of animals used also rose by 727 to 2,186.

Species on which no procedures were started in 2012

No procedures were performed using greyhounds, a number of primate species, camelids, other ungulates[26], quail (Coturnix coturnix)[27] and Octopus vulgaris[28]. No great apes have been used since the current legislation (the 1986 Act) was implemented in 1987.

Source
(Table 2 and online Supplementary Tables 2.1, 2.2)

The majority (82% or 3.37 million) of the 4.11 million procedures started in 2012 were performed using animals listed in Schedule 2 of the Act. These animals must come from a designated source[29], unless a special exemption is granted. Animals listed in Schedule 2 are: mice; rats; guinea pigs; hamsters; gerbils; rabbits; cats; dogs; ferrets; non-human primates; pigs (if genetically modified); sheep (if genetically modified); and common quail (Coturnix coturnix). The procedures involving animals listed in Schedule 2 and acquired from non-designated sources[30] in the UK are authorised under Section 10(3) of the Act. The following were sources for Schedule 2 listed animals in 2012:

- Designated establishments in the UK were the source of animals for 3.35 million (82%) procedures using Schedule 2 listed species.

- Other EU countries were the source of animals for 11,900 (0.3%) procedures using Schedule 2 listed species.

- Schedule 2 listed animals acquired from other sources (including Council of Europe countries who are signatories to ETS123[31]) were used in 16,000 procedures (0.4%).

---

[26] Ungulates are animals which have hooves.
[27] Coturnix coturnix is the common quail. Quail (not Coturnix coturnix) refers to all other species of quail.
[28] Octopus vulgaris refers to the common Octopus.
[29] A designated source is a supplier licensed to breed or supply animals for scientific purposes.
[30] Non-designated sources include any unlicensed source of animals in the UK, as well as any source of animals outside of the UK.
[31] European Convention for the Protection of Vertebrate Animals used for Experimental and Other Scientific Purposes.

Genetic status
(Table 3 and online Supplementary Tables 3 (full), 3.1, 3.2, 3.3)

Figure 6 below shows the number of procedures performed by the genetic status of the animal between 1995 and 2012. It shows that the use of GM animals increased considerably over the period from 215,300 in 1995 to 1.91 million animals in 2012 (+1.69 million or +786%), with the breeding of GM animals and fundamental biological research being the main primary purposes accounting for the rise. In 2012, for the first time in the series, the number of procedures involving GM animals was greater than the number involving normal animals[32].

Between 1995 and 2012, the number of procedures involving animals with a harmful genetic mutation also rose, but to a lesser extent, from 226,600 in 1995 to 525,000 in 2012 (+298,400 or +132%), with the breeding of HM animals driving the increase. The change between 2011 and 2012 accounted for half of this increase (+149,300).

Over the same period, the use of normal animals decreased from 2.27 million in 1995 to 1.68 million in 2012 (-591,200 or -26%), mainly due to a reduction in procedures undertaken for applied studies, although there was an increase in the use of normal animals for the breeding of GM or HM animals.

Figure 6: Procedures by genetic status of animal, 1995–2012

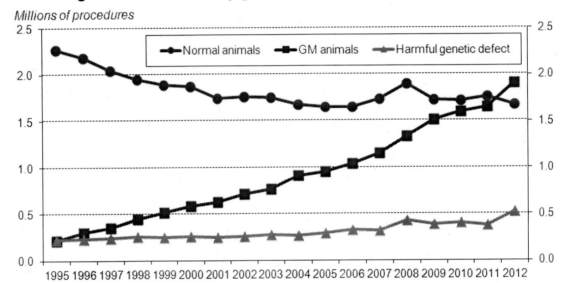

Genetically normal animals

There were 1.68 million procedures involving normal animals in 2012 (41% of the overall total), with mice, fish and rats accounting for the majority (52%, 17%, and 15% of normal animals respectively), and fundamental biological research, applied studies and the breeding of GM or HM animals being the main primary purposes for these species. Compared with 2011, there was a decrease in procedures using normal animals (-86,900 or -5%), mainly due to a decline in the use of fish (-117,000 or -29%), although there was an increase in the use of mice (+46,400 or +6%).

Animals with a harmful genetic mutation

There were 525,000 procedures involving animals with a harmful genetic mutation in 2012 (13% of the overall total), with mice accounting for the majority (84% of animals with a harmful genetic mutation) , and the breeding of HM animals being the main primary purpose for this species. Compared with

[32] Non-GM or HM animals.

2011, there was an increase in procedures using animals with a harmful genetic mutation (+149,300 or +40%), which was also mainly attributable to mice (+119,100 or +37%).

<u>Genetically modified animals</u>

There were 1.91 million procedures involving GM animals in 2012 (46% of the overall total), with mice accounting for the majority (91% of GM animals), and breeding of GM animals and fundamental biological research being the main primary purposes for this species. Compared with 2011, there was an increase in procedures using GM animals (+254,800 or +15%), with mice also being the key driver of the increase (+213,500 or 14%).

Target body system
(Table 4)

In 2012, 2.12 million, slightly over half (52%) of all procedures, were directed towards one particular body system[33].

- The immune system was the largest single category, accounting for 557,400 procedures (14% of all procedures), of which the main species used was mice (514,200 or 92% of this type of procedure).

- The nervous and reproductive systems were the next largest single categories with 417,900 (10%) and 356,700 (9%) procedures respectively. Mice, rats and fish were the most common species used for these systems accounting for 415,600 (99%) of procedures for the former and 341,100 (96%) of procedures for the latter.

- Of the single body system categories, the largest increase was in the alimentary[34] body system (+108,000 or +167%) and the largest decrease was in the respiratory system (-27,400 or -24%).

Procedures conducted where the target body system was not relevant accounted for 836,300 (20% of all procedures) and remained stable compared with 2011 (-4,200 or -0%). The category for multiple target body systems accounted for 1.16 million procedures (28% of all procedures) increasing by 171,900 (+17%).

Use of anaesthesia
(Table 5)

Procedures which cause pain, suffering, distress, or lasting harm to the animal are only permitted without anaesthesia[35] or analgesic[36] when such administration is judged more traumatic than the procedure itself, or when it is incompatible with the object of the procedure.

- In 2012, 28 per cent of procedures (1.16 million) had some form of anaesthesia to alleviate the severity of the interventions, a similar proportion to 2011 (29%). For many of the remaining procedures the use of anaesthesia would have potentially increased the adverse effects of the procedure.

- The use of neuromuscular blocking agents (NMBA)[37] was recorded in 1,675 procedures, a decrease from 2,547 procedures in 2012. All NMBA procedures involved the use of general anaesthesia.

---

[33] A group of organs that work together to perform a certain task.
[34] Includes all parts of the body involved in preparing food for absorption into the body and excretion of waste products.
[35] Anaesthesia involves using medication to induce a loss of sensation in the animal.
[36] An analgesic is a drug used to relieve pain.
[37] Neuromuscular blocking agents (NMBA) relax skeletal muscles and induce paralysis.

Fundamental and applied studies other than toxicology, regulatory or safety purposes
(Table 6)

Non-toxicology[38] accounted for 3.73 million procedures in 2012 (91% of the total number of procedures), an increase of 339,200 (+10%) compared with the previous year. The main fields of research were: immunology (575,800 or 15% of the total number of non-toxicological procedures); cancer research (500,700 or 13%); physiology[39] (430,900 or 12%); anatomy[40] (430,400 or 12%); and genetics[41] (391,700 or 11%).

Compared with 2011, there were increases for: nutrition (+79,300 or +425%); anatomy (+73,200 or +20%); cancer research (+69,000 or +16%); genetics (+46,000 or +13%); ecology[42] (+33,100 or +85%); and biochemistry[43] (+15,800 or +54%). There were falls for: physiology (-173,600 or -29%); pharmaceutical research and development (-24,600 or -11%); and pharmacology[44] (-10,100 or -14%).

Production of biological materials
(Table 7)

In 2012, 357,800 procedures were carried out to produce biological materials, 8,100 more (+2%) than in 2011. Biological materials were produced for the following purposes:

- 134,500 procedures (38% of the procedures undertaken to produce biological materials) were for the production of infectious agents, of which the most common species used were birds (78%) and mice 17%).

- Vectors[45], neoplasms[46] and antibody production[47] accounted for 30,600 procedures (9%) undertaken to produce biological materials, with mice predominantly used (87%).

- The remaining 192,700 biological procedures (54%) were undertaken to produce other biological material such as tissues or blood products, with mice (65%) and pigs, sheep, and all other ungulates (19%) used.

- The numbers of procedures using immunisation to produce monoclonal antibodies by in vitro methods fell by 17 per cent (-300) to 1,600 procedures in 2012, less than half the level of 4,000 procedures in 2008.

Toxicology, other safety or efficacy evaluation
(Tables 9, 9a, 10, 11; online Supplementary Tables 12, 15, 16; and online Time Series Table 25)

In 2012, 377,000 procedures were undertaken for toxicological or other safety/efficacy[48] evaluation

---

[38] For the purposes of these statistics, toxicology means the safety evaluation of the effects of substances on man, animals or the environment, mainly medical treatments.

[39] The study of the functions of the individual structures and systems within an organism.

[40] The study of a physical structure of an organism.

[41] The study of genes, heredity, and variation in living organisms.

[42] The study of interactions among organisms and their environment.

[43] The study of chemical processes within, and relating to, living organisms.

[44] The study of drugs.

[45] A vector is an agent that transfers genetic material from one cell to another.

[46] A neoplasm is an abnormal growth of tissue in animals.

[47] Antibodies identify and neutralise foreign objects such as bacteria and viruses.

[48] Safety testing is generally carried out to meet regulatory requirements for safety of pharmaceuticals, chemicals etc. Efficacy testing is to demonstrate the effectiveness of drugs, which may or may not be carried out for regulatory purposes.

purposes, nine per cent of the total 4.11 million procedures. This represents a decrease of 22,100 (-6%) compared with 2011, which continues the overall trend of a fall in toxicological procedures in recent years. The decrease in 2012 was mainly attributable to a decline in the use of fish (-41,600 or -55%) but there was also a rise in the use of mice (+16,400 or +10%). In 2012, 281,700 (75%) of toxicological procedures were for pharmaceutical safety/efficacy evaluation, with 223,100 involving mice or rats (79% of all pharmaceutical safety/efficacy evaluation procedures) and just 2,100 (less than 1%) involving non-human primates. Following a Government ban, no toxicological procedures involving cosmetics have been undertaken on animals since 1998.

Figure 7 shows the toxicological procedures undertaken by species of animal in 2012. Mice were the main species used with 184,000 procedures (49% of the toxicological total). Rats and fish were the next most common species, accounting for 111,500 (30%) and 34,700 (9%) of toxicological procedures respectively. Other species used were birds[49] (17,700 or 5% of the toxicology total), rabbits (10,000 or 3%), other animals[50] (9,600 or 3%) and all other rodents[51] (9,400 or 2%).

[49] Includes domestic fowl (Gallus domesticus), quail, and other bird species. The species are grouped together for the purposes of the pie chart but data are collected and published on them separately.
[50] Includes dogs (beagles), other carnivores, horses and other equids, pigs, goats, sheep, cattle, marmosets/ tamarins, macaques, and amphibians. The species are grouped together for the purposes of the pie chart but data are collected and published on them separately.
[51] Includes guinea pigs, hamsters, gerbils, and other rodent species. The species are grouped together for the purposes of the pie chart but data are collected and published on them separately.

Figure 7: Procedures (toxicology) by species of animal, 2012

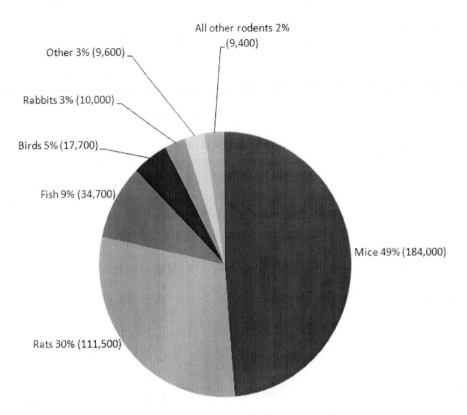

All other rodents 2% (9,400)

Other 3% (9,600)

Rabbits 3% (10,000)

Birds 5% (17,700)

Fish 9% (34,700)

Mice 49% (184,000)

Rats 30% (111,500)

Figure 8 shows that the majority of toxicological procedures (353,200 or 94%) conformed to legal or regulatory requirements with most (314,100 or 83%) meeting a combination of requirements. In 2012, 23,900 (6%) procedures did not conform to any legislative requirements.

Figure 8: Procedures by legislative requirement (toxicology), 2012

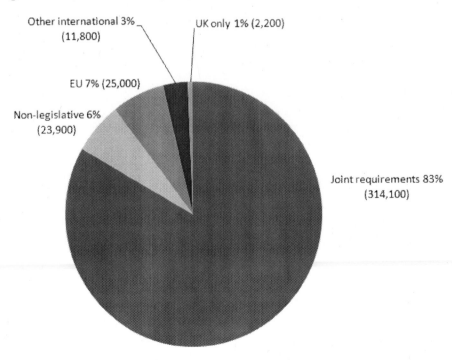

Other international 3% (11,800)

UK only 1% (2,200)

EU 7% (25,000)

Non-legislative 6% (23,900)

Joint requirements 83% (314,100)

Rodenticide trials

It is impracticable to collect accurate figures on the number of animals used in field trials of rodenticide[52] substances. Nonetheless, no returns indicated that such field trials occurred in 2012.

Use of animals on the CITES list

Returns were required on the use of animals listed in Appendix 1 of the Convention on International Trade in Endangered Species of Flora and Fauna (CITES)[53] or in Annex C.1 to the Council Regulation (EEC) 3626/82 (see form notes section in the User Guide). There were 147 procedures performed using animals in this category in 2012; these involved wild birds and amphibia in research relevant to those species.

Type of establishment
(Table 19 and Online Time Series Table 23)

Universities accounted for the majority of procedures in 2012, undertaking 48 per cent (1.97 million) of the 4.11 million procedures. In addition, universities held 76 per cent (2,467) of the 3,239 licences for which returns were received. Other types of establishment which undertook procedures were commercial organisations (accounting for 27% or 1.13 million procedures), other public bodies (accounting for 13% or 549,500 procedures) and non-profit organisations (accounting for 9% or 352,000 procedures). These organisations respectively held eight per cent, seven per cent and four per cent of the licences for which returns were received.

Figure 9 shows the procedures undertaken in universities/medical schools and commercial organisations between 1995 and 2012. The number of procedures accounted for by the commercial sector decreased between 1995 and 2005 from 1.33 million to 908,200 (-421,200 or -32%). The figure then rose from then on to 1.33 million in 2008, the same figure as 1995, and then fell in the following year to 1.03 million. The number remained relatively stable between 2009 and 2011 and then increased slightly in 2012 to 1.13 million. Between 1995 and 2012, the number of procedures carried out in the university sector rose by 1.14 million (+139%) to 1.97 million, with the figure overtaking the commercial sector from 2002 onwards.

The difference in trends between the commercial sector and the university sector is likely to reflect the increase in fundamental research using GM animals within universities, as well as the decline in procedures undertaken for toxicological purposes.

---

[52] Rodenticides are a category of pest control chemicals intended to kill rodents. Rodenticide trials are field trials of such chemicals and are occasionally undertaken by commercial companies who produce them.
[53] CITES is an international agreement between governments with the aim of ensuring that international trade in specimens of wild animals and plants does not threaten their survival.

Figure 9: Procedures by establishment type, 1995–2012

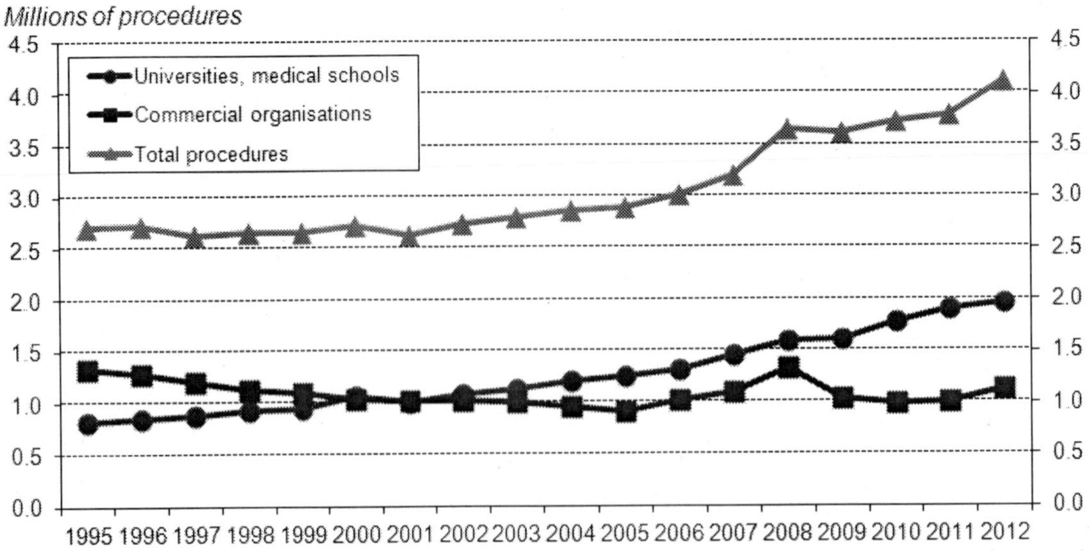

Millions of procedures

International comparisons
(Table 1a and Commission report[54] Tables 1.0 and 1.1)

Data compiled by EU countries and submitted to the European Commission use a narrower, but common, definition of animal experiments. The main difference with the definition used for the other statistics in this publication is that the data are based on numbers of animals and excludes breeding to produce GM or HM animals. The latest data are for 2008[55] and some of the key points are as follows:

- The total number of animals used for experiments in the 27 EU Member States in 2008 was just over 12 million, falling by two per cent compared with 2005.

- In France, the UK and Germany there were experiments using 2.33 million animals, 2.27 million animals, and 2.02 million animals respectively.

- No apes were used in experiments anywhere in the EU in 2008. A total of 9,569 non-human primates were used in experiments across the EU27, a third (35% or 3,354) of which were used in the UK.

The full report is available on the Commission's website
http://ec.europa.eu/environment/chemicals/lab_animals/reports_en.htm

Returns, project licensees and designated places
(Appendix A Table 19)

Statistical returns are required each year from every person in Great Britain who holds a project licence for part or all of the year. For 2012, 3,239 licensees provided returns which reported either that

---

[54] Commission Staff Working Paper - Report on the Statistics on the Number of Animals used for Experimental and other Scientific Purposes in the Member States of the European Union in the year 2008 (SEC (2010) 1107/final 2), available at http://ec.europa.eu/environment/chemicals/lab_animals/reports_en.htm. Data quoted are from Tables 1.0 and 1.1 of the Commission Working Paper SEC (2010) 1107/final 2, available at http://ec.europa.eu/environment/chemicals/lab_animals/pdf/sec_2010_1107.pdf.

[55] Data for France related to 2007.

procedures were started (2,556 licensees, of which 15 reported only non-countable procedures[56]) or that none were started (681 licensees).

There were 2,717 project licences in force at the end of 2012 compared with 2,624 at the end of 2011, a slight increase. The number of certificates of designation in force authorising places where work was carried out was 176 at the end of 2012 compared with 181 at the end of 2011, continuing the trend of falls in recent years. The number of personal licences in force decreased to 14,875 at the end of 2012, compared with 15,403 at the end of 2011.

Further information

Information about research and testing using animals can be found at https://www.gov.uk/research-and-testing-using-animals.

Information about the Animals in Science Committee can be found at https://www.gov.uk/government/organisations/animals-in-science-committee.

Information about the National Centre for the Replacement, Refinement and Reduction of Animals in research (NC3Rs) can be found at http://www.nc3rs.org.uk/.

Information relating to Northern Ireland is published by the Department of Health, Social Services and Public Safety and can be found at http://www.dhsspsni.gov.uk/healthprotection-animalscience.

Information on public attitudes to animal testing is available from IPSOS MORI at http://www.ipsos-mori.com/researchpublications/publications/1343/Views-on-Animal-Experimentation.aspx.

Tables

Notes providing details of the terms and classifications used ('User Guide to Home Office Statistics of Scientific Procedures on Living Animals'), and the 'Supplementary Tables' and 'Time Series Tables' can be found at: https://www.gov.uk/government/publications/statistics-of-scientific-procedures-on-living-animals-great-britain-2012.

Definitions

All tables refer to the numbers of scientific procedures started on adult animals in 2012, unless indicated otherwise. Tables suffixed with an 'a' (e.g. Tables 1a, 6a, 9a) relate to the numbers of animals used.

Symbols used in tables

..	not available	-	nil
NA	not applicable	r	revised

---

[56] It is not possible to collect accurate figures on the numbers of procedures started using immature forms (e.g. larvae, embryos). Information is collected indicating when procedures using such forms are carried out, which are classified as non-countable procedures.

Organisation Chart: Relationship between the tables, 2012

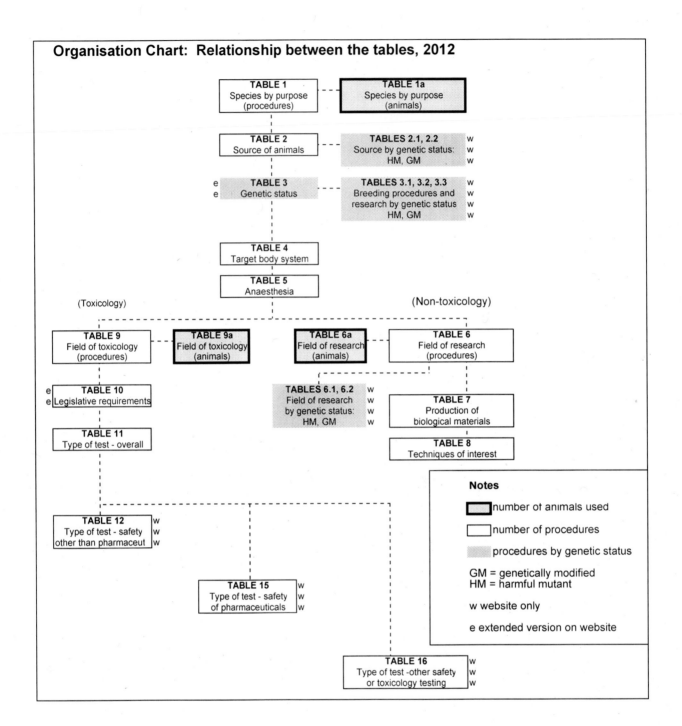

TABLE 1
Species by purpose
(procedures)

TABLE 1a
Species by purpose
(animals)

TABLE 2
Source of animals

TABLES 2.1, 2.2   w
Source by genetic status: w
HM, GM   w

e   TABLE 3
e   Genetic status

TABLES 3.1, 3.2, 3.3   w
Breeding procedures and   w
research by genetic status   w
HM, GM   w

TABLE 4
Target body system

TABLE 5
Anaesthesia

(Toxicology)

(Non-toxicology)

TABLE 9
Field of toxicology
(procedures)

TABLE 9a
Field of toxicology
(animals)

TABLE 6a
Field of research
(animals)

TABLE 6
Field of research
(procedures)

e   TABLE 10
e   Legislative requirements

TABLES 6.1, 6.2   w
Field of research   w
by genetic status: w
HM, GM   w

TABLE 7
Production of
biological materials

TABLE 11
Type of test - overall

TABLE 8
Techniques of interest

TABLE 12
Type of test - safety   w
other than pharmaceut   w
w

TABLE 15
Type of test - safety   w
of pharmaceuticals   w
w

TABLE 16
Type of test -other safety   w
or toxicology testing   w
w

Notes

number of animals used

number of procedures

procedures by genetic status

GM = genetically modified
HM = harmful mutant

w website only

e extended version on website

Table 1 Scientific procedures by species of animal and primary purpose of the procedure, page 1 of 2

Great Britain 2012

Species of animal	Primary purpose of the procedure									Number of procedures
	Fundamental biological research	Applied studies -human medicine or dentistry	Applied studies -veterinary medicine	Protection of man, animals or environment	Education	Training	Forensic enquiries	Direct diagnosis	Breeding of GM or HM animals	Total
Mammal										
Mouse	902,799	345,173	15,916	13,738	889	10	-	3,390	1,776,906	3,058,821
Rat	75,477	119,520	192	51,264	415	693	-	4	30,821	278,386
Guinea pig	1,611	9,788	1,148	-	110	-	-	83	-	12,740
Hamster	880	1,323	-	33	-	-	-	-	-	2,236
Gerbil	340	-	-	-	-	-	-	-	-	340
Other rodent	2,652	-	-	361	-	-	-	-	-	3,013
Rabbit	978	7,930	2,401	1,445	16	-	-	1,069	27	13,866
Cat	107	-	140	-	-	-	-	-	-	247
Dog	-	-	-	-	-	-	-	-	-	-
Beagle	334	3,952	255	102	-	-	-	-	-	4,643
Greyhound	-	-	-	-	-	-	-	-	-	-
Other including cross-bred dogs	130	-	68	-	-	-	-	-	2	200
Ferret	125	201	4	-	13	-	-	5	-	348
Other carnivore	529	-	49	135	-	-	-	-	-	713
Horse and other equids	115	-	298	-	-	-	-	8,069	-	8,482
Pig	779	709	1,768	23	-	-	-	-	100	3,379
Goat	20	5	1,607	16	-	-	-	10	-	1,658
Sheep	4,602	527	1,183	132	-	-	-	36,369	58	42,871
Cattle	4,056	-	1,274	73	-	-	-	79	-	5,482
Deer	77	-	-	-	-	-	-	-	-	77
Camelid	-	-	-	-	-	-	-	-	-	-
Other ungulate	-	-	-	-	-	-	-	-	-	-

Table 1 Scientific procedures by species of animal and primary purpose of the procedure, page 2 of 2

Great Britain 2012

Number of procedures

Species of animal	Fundamental biological research	Applied studies - human medicine or dentistry	Applied studies - veterinary medicine	Protection of man, animals or environment	Education	Training	Forensic enquiries	Direct diagnosis	Breeding of GM or HM animals	Total
Primate										
Prosimian	-	-	-	-	-	-	-	-	-	-
New World monkey										
marmoset, tamarin	177	106	-	-	-	-	-	-	-	**283**
Squirrel, owl, spider monkey	-	-	-	-	-	-	-	-	-	-
Other New World monkey	-	-	-	-	-	-	-	-	-	-
Old World monkey										
Macaque	181	2,412	-	120	-	-	-	24	-	**2,737**
Baboon	-	-	-	-	-	-	-	-	-	-
Other Old World monkey	-	-	-	-	-	-	-	-	-	-
Ape										
Gibbon	-	-	-	-	-	-	-	-	-	-
Great ape	-	-	-	-	-	-	-	-	-	-
Other mammal	533	-	-	-	-	-	-	-	-	**533**
Bird										
Domestic fowl (*Gallus domesticus*)	5,758	271	128,499	281	-	-	-	1,053	1,197	**137,059**
Turkey	800	154	3,292	-	-	-	-	190	-	**4,436**
Quail (*Coturnix coturnix*)	308	-	-	550	-	-	-	-	-	**858**
Quail (not *Coturnix coturnix*)	-	-	-	-	-	-	-	-	-	-
Other bird	9,718	-	-	1,293	-	-	-	569	-	**11,580**
Reptile - any reptilian species	513	-	-	-	-	-	-	-	-	**513**
Amphibian - any amphibian species	11,118	-	-	404	-	-	-	-	2,175	**13,697**
Fish - any fish species	279,375	3,623	18,276	29,811	70	-	-	-	169,675	**500,830**
Cephalopod - *Octopus vulgaris*	-	-	-	-	-	-	-	-	-	-
Total	**1,304,092**	**495,694**	**176,370**	**99,781**	**1,513**	**703**	-	**50,914**	**1,980,961**	**4,110,028**
Increase on 2011	-34,781	12,899	-10,643	-17,035	32	-17	-23	3,591	363,148	317,171
Percentage change from 2011	-3%	3%	-6%	-15%	2%	-2%	N/A	8%	22%	8%
Percentage of total for 2012	32%	12%	4%	2%	0.0%	0.0%	0.0%	1%	48%	100%
2011 Totals	1,338,873	482,795	187,013	116,816	1,481	720	23	47,323	1,617,813	3,792,857

Primary purpose of the procedure

N/A = Not applicable

26

Table 1a Animals used, by species of animal and primary purpose of the procedure, page 1 of 2

Great Britain 2012

Species of animal	Primary purpose of the procedure								Number of animals
	Fundamental biological research	Applied studies -human medicine or dentistry	Applied studies -veterinary medicine	Protection of man, animals or environment	Education	Training	Forensic enquiries	Direct diagnosis	Breeding of GM or HM animals	Total
Mammal										
Mouse	897,620	343,707	15,916	13,730	889	10	-	3,390	1,774,694	3,049,956
Rat	72,520	117,435	192	50,970	415	693	-	4	30,817	273,046
Guinea pig	1,611	9,788	1,148	-	110	-	-	83	-	12,740
Hamster	880	1,323	-	33	-	-	-	-	-	2,236
Gerbil	327	-	-	-	-	-	-	-	-	327
Other rodent	1,684	-	-	361	-	-	-	-	-	2,045
Rabbit	807	5,561	1,663	1,445	16	-	-	1,019	27	10,538
Cat	62	-	140	-	-	-	-	-	-	202
Dog										
Beagle	139	2,647	247	85	-	-	-	-	-	3,118
Greyhound	-	-	-	-	-	-	-	-	-	-
Other including cross-bred dogs	26	-	68	-	-	-	-	-	2	96
Ferret	125	201	4	-	13	-	-	5	-	348
Other carnivore	481	-	27	135	-	-	-	-	-	643
Horse and other equids	23	-	125	-	-	-	-	43	-	191
Pig	758	639	1,610	21	-	-	-	-	97	3,125
Goat	20	5	1,607	16	-	-	-	10	-	1,658
Sheep	4,362	412	1,040	132	-	-	-	645	58	6,649
Cattle	3,404	-	1,216	67	-	-	-	79	-	4,766
Deer	77	-	-	-	-	-	-	-	-	77
Camelid	-	-	-	-	-	-	-	-	-	-
Other ungulate	-	-	-	-	-	-	-	-	-	-

Table 1a Animals used, by species of animal and primary purpose of the procedure, page 2 of 2

Great Britain 2012

Species of animal	Primary purpose of the procedure									Number of animals
	Fundamental biological research	Applied studies -human medicine or dentistry	Applied studies -veterinary medicine	Protection of man, animals or environment	Education	Training	Forensic enquiries	Direct diagnosis	Breeding of GM or HM animals	Total
Primate										
Prosimian	-	-	-	-	-	-	-	-	-	-
New World monkey										
marmoset, tamarin	171	61	-	-	-	-	-	-	-	232
Squirrel, owl, spider monkey	-	-	-	-	-	-	-	-	-	-
Other New World monkey	-	-	-	-	-	-	-	-	-	-
Old World monkey										
Macaque	97	1,739	-	115	-	-	-	3	-	1,954
Baboon	-	-	-	-	-	-	-	-	-	-
Other Old World monkey	-	-	-	-	-	-	-	-	-	-
Ape										
Gibbon	-	-	-	-	-	-	-	-	-	-
Great ape	-	-	-	-	-	-	-	-	-	-
Other mammal	460	-	-	-	-	-	-	-	-	460
Bird										
Domestic fowl (Gallus domesticus)	5,758	215	128,499	238	-	-	-	1,053	1,197	136,960
Turkey	800	10	3,292	-	-	-	-	82	-	4,184
Quail (Coturnix coturnix)	-	-	-	-	-	-	-	-	-	-
Quail (not Coturnix coturnix)	308	-	-	550	-	-	-	-	-	858
Other bird	8,816	-	-	1,293	-	-	-	248	-	10,357
Reptile - any reptilian species	513	-	-	-	-	-	-	-	-	513
Amphibian - any amphibian species	4,808	-	-	404	-	-	-	-	763	5,975
Fish - any fish species	279,050	3,623	18,276	29,811	70	-	-	-	169,226	500,056
Cephalopod - Octopus vulgaris	-	-	-	-	-	-	-	-	-	-
Total	1,285,707	487,366	175,070	99,406	1,513	703	-	6,664	1,976,881	4,033,310
Increase on 2011	-25,560	14,847	-10,418	-16,823	38	-17	-23	-2,273	362,918	322,689
Percentage change from 2011	-2%	3%	-6%	-14%	3%	-2%	N/A	-25%	22%	9%
Percentage of total for 2012	32%	12%	4%	2%	0.0%	0.0%	0.0%	0.2%	49%	100%
2011 Totals	1,311,267	472,519	185,488	116,229	1,475	720	23	8,937	1,613,963	3,710,621

N/A = Not applicable

28

Table 2 Scientific procedures by Schedule 2 listed species and source of animals

Great Britain 2012

Number of procedures

Species of animal	Source							Total
	Animals acquired from within own designated establishment	Animals acquired from another designated breeding or supplying establishment in the UK	Animals acquired from non-designated sources in the UK	Animals acquired from sources within the EU (outside the UK)	Animals acquired from Council of Europe countries who are signatories to ETS123	Animals acquired from other sources	Animals not listed in Schedule 2	
Mouse	2,466,003	573,594	329	7,296	384	11,215	-	3,058,821
Rat	62,385	213,444	14	1,366	-	1,177	-	278,386
Guinea pig	1,153	9,802	-	1,785	-	-	-	12,740
Hamster	339	1,641	-	256	-	-	-	2,236
Gerbil	266	17	-	33	-	24	-	340
Rabbit	4,972	8,236	-	325	-	333	-	13,866
Cat	72	2	-	92	-	81	-	247
Dog	1,259	2,297	39	641	-	607	-	4,843
Ferret	17	315	-	-	-	16	-	348
Pig (genetically modified)	43	-	-	-	-	-	-	43
Sheep (genetically modified)	33	-	-	-	-	-	-	33
Primate	409	342	-	80	-	2,189	-	3,020
Quail (Coturnix coturnix)	-	-	-	-	-	-	-	-
Animals not listed in Schedule 2	-	-	-	-	-	-	735,105	735,105
Total	2,536,951	809,690	382	11,874	384	15,642	735,105	4,110,028
Increase on 2011	373,484	12,351	-57	-1,777	228	1,869	-68,927	317,171
Percentage change from 2011	17%	2%	-13%	-13%	146%	14%	-9%	8%
Percentage of total for 2012	62%	20%	0.0%	0.3%	0.0%	0.4%	18%	100%
2011 Totals	2,163,467	797,339	439	13,651	156	13,773	804,032	3,792,857

Note. The total number of procedures using animals listed in schedule 2 was 3,374,923.

Table 3 Scientific procedures by species of animal, and genetic status
Summary Version

Note. For numbers of procedures by purpose, see full table available on the website

Great Britain 2012   **Number of procedures**

Species of animal	Genetic status			Total
	Normal animal	Animal with harmful genetic mutation	Genetically modified animal	
Mammal				
Mouse	875,298	441,610	1,741,913	3,058,821
Rat	243,954	27,386	7,046	278,386
Guinea pig	12,740	-	-	12,740
Hamster	2,236	-	-	2,236
Gerbil	340	-	-	340
Other rodent	3,013	-	-	3,013
Rabbit	13,839	-	27	13,866
Cat	247	-	-	247
Dog				
Beagle	4,643	-	-	4,643
Greyhound	-	-	-	-
Other inc cross-breds	198	2	-	200
Ferret	348	-	-	348
Other carnivore	713	-	-	713
Horse and other equids	8,482	-	-	8,482
Pig	3,336	-	43	3,379
Goat	1,658	-	-	1,658
Sheep	42,838	-	33	42,871
Cattle	5,482	-	-	5,482
Deer	77	-	-	77
Camelid	-	-	-	-
Other ungulate	-	-	-	-
Primate				
Prosimian	-	-	-	-
New World monkey				
marmoset, tamarin	283	-	-	283
Squirrel, owl, spider monkey	-	-	-	-
Other New World monkey	-	-	-	-
Old World monkey				
Macaque	2,737	-	-	2,737
Baboon	-	-	-	-
Other Old World monkey	-	-	-	-
Ape				
Gibbon	-	-	-	-
Great ape	-	-	-	-
Other mammal	533	-	-	533
Bird				
Domestic fowl (*Gallus domesticus*)	135,836	522	701	137,059
Turkey	4,436	-	-	4,436
Quail (*Coturnix coturnix*)	-	-	-	-
Quail (not *Coturnix coturnix*)	858	-	-	858
Other bird	11,580	-	-	11,580
Reptile	513	-	-	513
Amphibian	11,179	405	2,113	13,697
Fish	289,131	55,056	156,643	500,830
Cephalopod	-	-	-	-
Total	**1,676,528**	**524,981**	**1,908,519**	**4,110,028**
Percentage of total for 2012	41%	13%	46%	100%

Table 4 Scientific procedures by species of animal and target body system

Great Britain 2012

Number of procedures

Species of animal	Body systems												Total
	Respiratory	Cardiovascular	Nervous	Senses	Alimentary	Skin	Musculo-skeletal	Reproductive	Immune and reticulo-endothelial	Other system	Multiple systems	System not relevant	
Mammal													
Mouse	57,674	103,371	298,605	40,541	61,269	42,194	51,523	244,521	514,229	67,239	963,624	614,031	**3,058,821**
Rat	21,162	14,165	64,542	2,484	4,138	464	1,616	38,107	7,124	3,183	61,725	59,676	**278,386**
All other rodents	2,439	3,068	241	310	283	525	-	34	5,797	-	3,276	2,356	**18,329**
Rabbit	60	823	9	187	4	715	54	1,527	2,954	694	4,977	1,862	**13,866**
Cat	-	32	14	6	3	-	-	-	3	-	133	56	**247**
Dog	132	359	-	-	99	-	2	25	44	129	1,844	2,209	**4,843**
Ferret	96	13	-	52	-	-	-	-	40	-	9	138	**348**
Other carnivore	-	3	-	-	-	-	-	94	-	-	33	583	**713**
Horse and other equids	87	71	-	-	-	-	2	17	129	6,363	96	1,712	**8,482**
Pig	159	87	95	-	280	56	-	142	918	84	607	951	**3,379**
Sheep	262	234	164	-	899	159	213	423	1,196	33,076	2,989	3,256	**42,871**
All other ungulates	325	31	4	-	1,760	-	-	1,048	2,434	294	1,266	55	**7,217**
New World monkey	-	7	30	-	-	-	-	-	-	-	153	93	**283**
Old World monkey	35	30	59	2	-	-	-	20	86	-	809	1,696	**2,737**
All other mammals	-	-	-	5	-	81	-	101	-	-	-	346	**533**
Bird	640	1,296	1,483	504	9,748	-	301	2,635	6,085	112,545	10,587	8,109	153,933
Reptile	-	-	-	-	-	-	-	-	-	513	-	-	**513**
Amphibian	-	-	167	-	119	383	221	9,510	-	-	1,189	2,108	**13,697**
Fish	4,580	13,087	52,441	4,925	93,952	9,803	7,195	58,498	16,403	1,200	101,688	137,058	500,830
Total	**87,651**	**136,677**	**417,854**	**49,016**	**172,554**	**54,385**	**61,127**	**356,702**	**557,442**	**225,320**	**1,155,005**	**836,295**	**4,110,028**
Increase on 2011	-27,419	4,373	-2,273	-2,154	107,994	-2,761	17,146	32,808	44,876	-23,071	171,854	-4,202	317,171
Percentage change from 2011	-24%	3%	-1%	-4%	167%	-5%	39%	10%	9%	-9%	17%	-0.5%	8%
Percentage of total for 2012	2%	3%	10%	1%	4%	1%	1%	9%	14%	5%	28%	20%	100%
2011 Totals	115,070	132,304	420,127	51,170	64,560	57,146	43,981	323,894	512,566	248,391	983,151	840,497	3,792,857

Table 5 Scientific procedures by species of animal and level of anaesthesia

Great Britain 2012

Species of animal	No anaesthesia	Type of anaesthesia				Number of procedures
		General anaesthesia, with recovery	Local anaesthesia	General anaesthesia at end of procedure, without recovery	General anaesthesia throughout, without recovery	Total
Mammal						
Mouse	2,363,943	419,004	130,951	97,120	47,803	3,058,821
Rat	161,015	69,349	881	26,935	20,206	278,386
All other rodents	11,725	2,629	141	1,604	2,230	18,329
Rabbit	8,334	325	1,517	1,389	2,301	13,866
Cat	94	153	-	-	-	247
Dog	3,898	402	124	274	145	4,843
Ferret	9	312	-	5	22	348
Other carnivore	220	477	-	-	16	713
Horse and other equids	350	12	8,120	-	-	8,482
Pig	2,659	347	12	1	360	3,379
Sheep	42,114	626	45	75	11	42,871
All other ungulates	7,129	16	68	-	4	7,217
Primate						
New World monkey	156	84	-	12	31	283
Old World monkey	2,004	716	-	5	12	2,737
All other mammals	528	3	-	-	2	533
Bird	50,234	635	-	101,989	1,075	153,933
Reptile	513	-	-	-	-	513
Amphibian	11,903	1,720	-	-	74	13,697
Fish	285,964	193,191	99	20,911	665	500,830
Total	**2,952,792**	**690,001**	**141,958**	**250,320**	**74,957**	**4,110,028**
Increase on 2011	257,071	131,534	-14,343	-54,311	-2,780	317,171
Percentage change from 2011	10%	24%	-9%	-18%	-4%	8%
Percentage of total for 2012	72%	17%	3%	6%	2%	100%
2011 Totals	2,695,721	558,467	156,301	304,631	77,737	3,792,857

Note. Neuromuscular blocking agents (NMBA) were used in 1,675 procedures in 2012. All of these procedures involved the use of general anaesthesia.

32

Table 6 Scientific procedures (non-toxicology) by species of animal and field of research, page 1 of 4

Great Britain 2012

Number of procedures

Species of animal	Field of research												
	Anatomy	Physiology	Biochemistry	Psychology	Pathology	Immunology	Microbiology	Parasitology	Pharmacology	Pharmaceutical R&D	Therapeutics	Clinical medicine	Clinical surgery
Mammal													
Mouse	272,811	363,470	43,166	28,479	65,581	553,265	29,491	29,669	40,363	116,757	17,167	17,663	1,472
Rat	5,369	33,168	509	8,791	2,031	2,791	927	655	16,749	58,310	3,681	3,451	1,068
Guinea pig	-	378	-	-	21	265	239	-	1,648	1,836	101	-	-
Hamster	-	212	4	-	-	45	325	185	-	172	78	-	-
Gerbil	-	5	-	-	-	1	-	294	-	-	40	-	-
Other rodent	-	-	-	-	19	-	-	2,383	-	-	-	-	-
Rabbit	5	559	157	-	33	929	336	-	48	1,678	32	51	32
Cat	-	2	-	-	-	59	-	2	61	-	6	-	-
Dog													
Beagle	-	-	-	-	-	105	-	-	24	710	-	-	-
Greyhound	-	-	-	-	-	-	-	-	-	-	-	-	-
Other including cross-bred dogs	-	3	-	-	-	-	-	-	-	-	2	-	-
Ferret	3	28	-	21	-	-	274	-	13	9	-	-	-
Other carnivore	17	5	-	94	-	-	-	-	10	-	-	-	-
Horse and other equids	103	203	-	-	130	72	8,103	26	76	-	-	69	14
Pig	-	-	-	109	-	349	97	-	23	63	102	95	43
Goat	-	-	-	-	-	10	10	-	-	47	-	-	-
Sheep	83	394	189	138	82	690	35,907	855	-	177	28	339	159
Cattle	-	1,115	-	-	4	1,586	112	145	4	280	-	-	-
Deer	-	-	-	-	-	-	-	-	-	-	-	-	-
Camelid	-	-	-	-	-	-	-	-	-	-	-	-	-
Other ungulate	-	-	-	-	-	-	-	-	-	-	-	-	-

Table 6 Scientific procedures (non-toxicology) by species of animal and field of research, page 2 of 4

Great Britain 2012

Number of procedures

Species of animal	Anatomy	Physiology	Biochemistry	Psychology	Pathology	Immunology	Microbiology	Parasitology	Pharmacology	Pharmaceutical R&D	Therapeutics	Clinical medicine	Clinical surgery
							Field of research						
Primate													
Prosimian	-	-	-	-	-	-	-	-	-	-	-	-	-
New World monkey													
marmoset, tamarin	7	48	-	38	59	13	4	-	25	47	-	-	-
Squirrel, owl, spider monkey	-	-	-	-	-	-	-	-	-	-	-	-	-
Other New World monkey	-	-	-	-	-	-	-	-	-	-	-	-	-
Old World monkey													
Macaque	3	18	56	40	-	74	64	-	-	214	-	-	-
Baboon	-	-	-	-	-	-	-	-	-	-	-	-	-
Other Old World monkey	-	-	-	-	-	-	-	-	-	-	-	-	-
Ape													
Gibbon	-	-	-	-	-	-	-	-	-	-	-	-	-
Great ape	-	-	-	-	-	-	-	-	-	-	-	-	-
Other mammal	-	5	-	-	-	-	-	-	-	-	-	-	-
Bird													
Domestic fowl (*Gallus domesticus*)	1,173	1,637	3	70	-	922	7,238	104,185	-	941	200	12	-
Turkey	-	-	-	-	-	18	222	1224	-	270	-	-	-
Quail (*Coturnix coturnix*)	-	-	-	-	-	-	-	-	-	-	-	-	-
Quail (not *Coturnix coturnix*)	-	241	-	-	-	-	-	-	-	-	-	-	-
Other bird	14	63	-	1,284	-	565	4	42	-	-	-	-	-
Reptile - any reptilian species	-	-	-	-	-	-	-	-	-	-	-	-	-
Amphibian - any amphibian species	10,680	476	1,057	-	-	-	303	80	24	-	-	-	-
Fish -any fish species	140,151	28,879	-	1,026	6,947	14,003	10,757	4,726	5,128	22,276	-	1,592	-
Cephalopod - Octopus vulgaris													
Total	430,419	430,909	45,141	40,090	74,907	575,762	94,413	144,471	64,196	203,787	21,437	23,272	2,788
Increase on 2011	73,166	-173,645	15,764	-6,096	1,248	43,661	6,918	-12,883	-10,127	-24,629	2,264	5,443	-236
Percentage change from 2011	20%	-29%	54%	-13%	2%	8%	8%	-8%	-14%	-11%	12%	31%	-8%
Percentage of total for 2012	12%	12%	1%	1%	2%	15%	3%	4%	2%	5%	1%	0.6%	0.1%
2011 Totals	357,253	604,554	29,377	46,186	73,659	532,101	87,495	157,354	74,323	228,416	19,173	17,829	3,024

Table 6 Scientific procedures (non-toxicology) by species of animal and field of research, page 3 of 4

Great Britain 2012

Number of procedures

Species of animal	Field of research													Total
	Dentistry	Genetics	Molecular biology	Cancer research	Nutrition	Zoology	Botany	Animal science	Ecology	Animal welfare	Other	Tobacco (1)	Alcohol	
Mammal														
Mouse	119	360,106	165,709	472,257	2,535	-	19	12	-	493	293,602	-	571	2,874,777
Rat	64	165	2,327	3,085	1,338	-	4	-	-	156	22,220	-	-	166,859
Guinea pig	-	-	-	-	-	-	-	-	-	-	-	-	-	4,488
Hamster	-	-	131	20	80	-	-	-	-	-	-	-	-	1,252
Gerbil	-	-	-	-	-	-	-	-	-	-	-	-	-	340
Other rodent	-	-	-	-	-	-	-	-	441	-	-	-	-	2,843
Rabbit	-	-	-	-	-	-	6	-	-	-	12	-	-	3,878
Cat	-	32	-	-	85	-	-	-	-	-	-	-	-	247
Dog														
Beagle	-	-	-	-	-	-	-	-	-	6	-	-	-	845
Greyhound	-	-	-	-	-	-	-	-	-	-	-	-	-	-
Other including cross-bred dogs	-	-	19	46	130	-	-	-	-	-	-	-	-	200
Ferret	-	-	-	-	-	-	-	-	-	-	-	-	-	348
Other carnivore	-	-	-	-	-	46	-	-	524	-	1	-	-	675
Horse and other equids	-	-	-	-	20	-	-	-	-	-	-	-	-	8,376
Pig	-	-	-	6	-	-	-	70	-	-	25	-	-	1,444
Goat	-	1,565	10	-	-	-	-	-	-	-	-	-	-	1,642
Sheep	-	375	-	-	174	-	-	2,683	-	17	142	-	-	42,432
Cattle	-	-	-	-	110	-	-	1,535	-	-	-	-	-	4,891
Deer	-	77	-	-	-	-	-	-	-	-	-	-	-	77
Camelid	-	-	-	-	-	-	-	-	-	-	-	-	-	-
Other ungulate	-	-	-	-	-	-	-	-	-	-	-	-	-	-

(1) Following a Government decision in 1997, procedures using animals in research on tobacco have not been allowed.

Table 6 Scientific procedures (non-toxicology) by species of animal and field of research, page 4 of 4

Great Britain 2012

Number of procedures

Species of animal	Field of research													Total
	Dentistry	Genetics	Molecular biology	Cancer research	Nutrition	Zoology	Botany	Animal science	Ecology	Animal welfare	Other	Tobacco (1)	Alcohol	
Primate														
Prosimian	-	-		-		-	-	-	-	-	-	-		
New World monkey														
marmoset, tamarin	-	-		-		-	-	-	-	-	-	-		241
Squirrel, owl, spider monkey	-	-		-		-	-	-	-	-	-	-		-
Other New World monkey	-	-		-		-	-	-	-	-	-	-		-
Old World monkey														
Macaque	-	-		-		-	-	-	-	-	-	-		469
Baboon	-	-		-		-	-	-	-	-	-	-		-
Other Old World monkey	-	-		-		-	-	-	-	-	-	-		-
Ape														
Gibbon	-	-		-		-	-	-	-	-	-	-		-
Great ape	-	-		-		-	-	-	-	-	-	-		-
Other mammal	-	182		-		-	-	-	346	-	-	-		533
Bird														
Domestic fowl (*Gallus domesticus*)	-	-	63	-	390	-	-	5,110	-	101	-	-	-	122,045
Turkey	-	-	-	-	64	-	-	1,696	-	-	-	-	-	3,494
Quail (*Coturnix coturnix*)	-	-	-	-	-	-	-	-	-	-	-	-	-	-
Quail (not *Coturnix coturnix*)	-	-	-	-	-	67	-	-	-	-	-	-	-	308
Other bird	-	-	-	-	-	4,170	-	57	2,852	1,298	-	-	-	10,349
Reptile - any reptilian species	-	-	-	-	-	513	-	-	-	-	-	-	-	513
Amphibian - any amphibian species	-	593	20	51	-	-	9	-	-	-	-	-	-	13,293
Fish - any fish species	-	28,571	12,401	25,214	92,984	1,162	-	-	67,946	857	-	-	1,500	466,120
Cephalopod - *Octopus vulgaris*	-	-	-	-	-	-	-	-	-	-	-	-	-	-
Total	**183**	**391,666**	**180,680**	**500,679**	**97,910**	**5,958**	**38**	**11,163**	**72,109**	**2,928**	**316,002**	**-**	**2,071**	**3,732,979**
Increase on 2011	102	45,972	385	69,022	79,261	878	4	2,501	33,120	1,255	184,370	-	1,530	339,248
Percentage change from 2011	126%	13%	0.2%	16%	425.0%	17%	12%	29%	85%	75%	140%	N/A	283%	10%
Percentage of total for 2012	0.0%	10%	5%	13%	2.6%	0.2%	0.0%	0.3%	2%	0.1%	8%	0%	0.1%	100%
2011 Totals	81	345,694	180,295	431,657	18,649	5,080	34	8,662	38,989	1,673	131,632	0	541	3,393,731

(1) Following a Government decision in 1997, procedures using animals in research on tobacco have not been allowed.

N/A = Not applicable

36

Table 6a Animals used (non-toxicology), by species of animal and field of research, page 1 of 4

Great Britain 2012

Number of animals

Species of animal	Field of research												
	Anatomy	Physiology	Biochemistry	Psychology	Pathology	Immunology	Microbiology	Parasitology	Pharmacology	Pharmaceutical Research and Development	Therapeutics	Clinical medicine	Clinical surgery
Mammal													
Mouse	272,090	362,093	43,141	27,742	65,515	550,732	29,491	29,669	39,424	116,511	17,167	17,574	1,472
Rat	5,369	33,098	509	8,535	1,979	2,791	927	655	14,741	57,059	3,677	2,872	1,068
Guinea pig	-	378	-	-	21	265	239	-	1,648	1,836	101	-	-
Hamster	-	212	4	-	-	45	325	185	-	172	78	-	-
Gerbil	-	5	-	-	-	1	-	281	-	-	40	-	-
Other rodent	-	-	-	-	19	-	-	1,415	-	-	-	-	-
Rabbit	5	559	29	-	33	886	286	-	48	1,670	32	51	32
Cat	-	2	-	-	-	59	-	2	49	-	6	-	-
Dog													
Beagle	-	-	-	-	-	105	-	-	10	185	-	-	-
Greyhound	-	-	-	-	-	-	-	-	-	-	-	-	-
Other including cross-bred dogs	-	3	-	-	-	-	-	-	-	-	2	-	-
Ferret	3	28	-	21	-	-	274	-	13	9	-	-	-
Other carnivore	-	-	-	46	-	-	-	-	-	-	-	-	-
Horse and other equids	3	5	-	-	-	12	43	-	4	-	-	-	11
Pig	103	188	-	100	130	214	97	26	23	63	102	95	43
Goat	-	-	-	-	-	10	10	-	-	47	-	-	-
Sheep	83	394	189	138	82	419	406	812	-	74	28	185	159
Cattle	-	1,115	-	-	4	1,558	112	145	4	280	-	-	-
Deer	-	-	-	-	-	-	-	-	-	-	-	-	-
Camelid	-	-	-	-	-	-	-	-	-	-	-	-	-
Other ungulate	-	-	-	-	-	-	-	-	-	-	-	-	-

Table 6a Animals used (non-toxicology), by species of animal and field of research, page 2 of 4

Great Britain 2012

Number of animals

Species of animal	Field of research												
	Anatomy	Physiology	Biochemistry	Psychology	Pathology	Immunology	Microbiology	Parasitology	Pharmacology	Pharmaceutical Research and Development	Therapeutics	Clinical medicine	Clinical surgery
Primate													
Prosimian	-	-	-	-	-	-	-	-	-	-	-	-	
New World monkey													
marmoset, tamarin	7	42	-	38	59	13	4	-	25	37	-	-	
Squirrel, owl, spider monkey	-	-	-	-	-	-	-	-	-	-	-	-	
Other New World monkey	-	-	-	-	-	-	-	-	-	-	-	-	
Old World monkey													
Macaque	2	18	2	11	-	74	64	-	-	6	-	-	
Baboon	-	-	-	-	-	-	-	-	-	-	-	-	
Other Old World monkey	-	-	-	-	-	-	-	-	-	-	-	-	
Ape													
Gibbon	-	-	-	-	-	-	-	-	-	-	-	-	
Great ape	-	-	-	-	-	-	-	-	-	-	-	-	
Other mammal	-	5	-	-	-	-	-	-	-	-	-	-	
Bird													
Domestic fowl (Gallus domesticus)	1,173	1,637	3	70	-	922	7,238	104,185	-	885	200	12	
Turkey	-	-	-	-	-	18	74	1,224	-	166	-	-	
Quail (Coturnix coturnix)	-	241	-	-	-	-	-	-	-	-	-	-	
Quail (not Coturnix coturnix)	-	-	-	-	-	-	-	-	-	-	-	-	
Other bird	14	63	-	1,199	-	248	-	42	-	-	-	-	
Reptile - any reptilian species	-	-	-	-	-	-	-	-	-	-	-	-	
Amphibian - any amphibian species	4,268	92	182	-	-	-	303	80	24	-	-	-	
Fish - any fish species	140,060	28,879	-	1,026	6,947	13,685	10,757	4,726	5,128	22,276	-	1,592	
Cephalopod - Octopus vulgaris	-	-	-	-	-	-	-	-	-	-	-	-	
Total	423,180	429,057	44,059	38,926	74,789	572,057	50,650	143,447	61,141	201,276	21,433	22,381	2,785

Table 6a Animals used (non-toxicology), by species of animal and field of research, page 3 of 4

Great Britain 2012

| Species of animal | Field of research | | | | | | | | | | | | | Number of animals |
	Dentistry	Genetics	Molecular biology	Cancer research	Nutrition	Zoology	Botany	Animal science	Ecology	Animal welfare	Other	Tobacco(1)	Alcohol	Total
Mammal														
Mouse	119	359,914	165,108	471,122	2,535	-	19	12	-	493	293,602	-	571	**2,866,116**
Rat	48	165	2,327	3,071	1,338	-	4	-	-	156	22,220	-	-	**162,609**
Guinea pig	-	-	-	-	-	-	-	-	-	-	-	-	-	**4,488**
Hamster	-	-	131	20	80	-	-	-	-	-	-	-	-	**1,252**
Gerbil	-	-	-	-	-	-	-	-	-	-	-	-	-	**327**
Other rodent	-	-	-	-	-	-	-	-	441	-	-	-	-	**1,875**
Rabbit	-	-	-	-	-	-	6	-	-	-	12	-	-	**3,649**
Cat	-	32	-	-	52	-	-	-	-	-	-	-	-	**202**
Dog														
Beagle	-	-	-	-	-	-	-	-	-	6	-	-	-	**306**
Greyhound	-	-	-	-	-	-	-	-	-	-	-	-	-	-
Other including cross-bred dogs	-	-	19	46	26	-	-	-	-	-	-	-	-	**96**
Ferret	-	-	-	-	-	-	-	-	-	-	-	-	-	**348**
Other carnivore	-	-	-	-	-	46	-	-	524	-	-	-	-	**616**
Horse and other equids	-	-	-	-	20	-	-	65	-	-	-	-	-	**98**
Pig	-	-	-	6	-	-	-	65	-	-	25	-	-	**1,280**
Goat	-	1,565	10	-	-	-	-	-	-	-	-	-	-	**1,642**
Sheep	-	375	-	-	83	-	-	2,636	-	17	142	-	-	**6,222**
Cattle	-	-	-	-	94	-	-	896	-	-	-	-	-	**4,208**
Deer	-	77	-	-	-	-	-	-	-	-	-	-	-	**77**
Camelid	-	-	-	-	-	-	-	-	-	-	-	-	-	-
Other ungulate	-	-	-	-	-	-	-	-	-	-	-	-	-	-

(1) Following a Government decision in 1997, procedures using animals in research on tobacco have not been allowed.

Table 6a Animals used (non-toxicology), by species of animal and field of research, page 4 of 4

Great Britain 2012

| Species of animal | Field of research | | | | | | | | | | | | | Number of animals |
	Dentistry	Genetics	Molecular biology	Cancer research	Nutrition	Zoology	Botany	Animal science	Ecology	Animal welfare	Other	Tobacco(1)	Alcohol	Total
Primate														
Prosimian	-	-	-	-	-	-	-	-	-	-	-	-	-	-
New World monkey														
marmoset, tamarin	-	-	-	-	-	-	-	-	-	-	-	-	-	225
Squirrel, owl, spider monkey	-	-	-	-	-	-	-	-	-	-	-	-	-	-
Other New World monkey	-	-	-	-	-	-	-	-	-	-	-	-	-	-
Old World monkey														
Macaque	-	-	-	-	-	-	-	-	-	-	-	-	-	177
Baboon	-	-	-	-	-	-	-	-	-	-	-	-	-	-
Other Old World monkey	-	-	-	-	-	-	-	-	-	-	-	-	-	-
Ape														
Gibbon	-	-	-	-	-	-	-	-	-	-	-	-	-	-
Great ape	-	-	-	-	-	-	-	-	-	-	-	-	-	-
Other mammal	-	182	-	-	-	-	-	-	273	-	-	-	-	460
Bird														
Domestic fowl (*Gallus domesticus*)	-	-	63	-	390	-	-	5,110	-	101	-	-	-	121,989
Turkey	-	-	-	-	64	-	-	1,696	-	-	-	-	-	3,242
Quail (*Coturnix coturnix*)	-	-	-	-	-	-	-	-	-	-	-	-	-	308
Quail (not *Coturnix coturnix*)	-	-	-	-	-	67	-	-	-	-	-	-	-	-
Other bird	-	-	-	-	-	3,476	-	1	2,785	1,298	-	-	-	9,126
Reptile - any reptilian species	-	-	-	-	-	513	-	-	-	-	-	-	-	513
Amphibian - any amphibian species	-	593	20	-	-	-	9	-	-	-	-	-	-	5,571
Fish - any fish species	-	28,531	12,401	25,214	92,659	1,162	-	-	67,946	857	-	-	1,500	465,346
Cephalopod - *Octopus vulgaris*	-	-	-	-	-	-	-	-	-	-	-	-	-	-
Total	167	391,434	180,079	499,479	97,341	5,264	38	10,416	71,969	2,928	316,001	-	2,071	3,662,368

(1) Following a Government decision in 1997, procedures using animals in research on tobacco have not been allowed

Table 7 Scientific procedures (non-toxicology) by species of animal and production of biological materials

Great Britain 2012

Species of animal	Production							Number of procedures	
	Infectious agents	Vectors	Neoplasms	Monoclonal antibodies (ascites model)	Monoclonal antibodies (initial immunisation)	Polyclonal antibodies	Other biological materials	Other [1]	Total
Mammal									
Mouse	23,478	3,747	13,933	-	1,467	7,480	126,180	2,698,492	**2,874,777**
Rat	669	65	249	-	43	61	10,751	155,021	**166,859**
All other rodents	349	-	20	-	-	81	1,155	7,318	**8,923**
Rabbit	-	-	-	-	28	2,200	793	857	**3,878**
Cat	2	-	-	-	-	3	-	242	**247**
Dog	-	-	-	-	-	-	677	368	**1,045**
Ferret	-	-	-	-	-	89	-	259	**348**
Other carnivore	-	-	-	-	-	-	3	672	**675**
Horse and other equids	-	-	-	-	-	1	6,426	1,949	**8,376**
Pigs, sheep & all other ungulates	661	3	-	-	24	855	36,440	12,503	**50,486**
Primate									
New World monkey	-	-	-	-	-	-	67	174	**241**
Old World monkey	-	-	-	-	-	-	289	180	**469**
All other mammals	-	-	-	-	-	-	-	533	**533**
Bird	104,411	-	-	-	-	243	2,032	29,510	**136,196**
Reptile, Amphibian	-	-	-	-	-	-	7,075	6,731	**13,806**
Fish	4,893	-	-	-	-	-	855	460,372	**466,120**
Total	**134,463**	**3,815**	**14,202**	**-**	**1,562**	**11,013**	**192,743**	**3,375,181**	**3,732,979**
Increase on 2011	-13,001	-1,354	3,668	0	-311	3,618	15,454	331,174	339,248
Percentage change from 2011	-9%	-26%	35%	N/A	-17%	49%	9%	11%	10.0%
Percentage of total for 2012	4%	0.1%	0.4%	0.0%	0.0%	0.3%	5%	90%	100%
2011 Totals	147,464	5,169	10,534	0	1,873	7,395	177,289	3,044,007	3,393,731

(1) Includes breeding procedures which are now detailed in Tables 3.1 - 3.3

N/A = Not applicable

41

Table 9 Scientific procedures (toxicology) by species of animal and toxicological purpose, page 1 of 4

Great Britain 2012 Number of procedures

Species of animal	Toxicology or other safety/efficacy evaluation							
	General safety/efficacy evaluation						Finished cosmetics(2)	Cosmetics ingredients (2)
	Pollution	Agriculture	Industry	Household	Food additives	Other foodstuffs		
Mammal								
Mouse	-	4,275	6,993	-	114	42	-	-
Rat	-	10,628	36,370	-	435	254	-	-
Guinea pig	-	-	-	-	-	-	-	-
Hamster	-	-	-	-	-	-	-	-
Gerbil	-	-	-	-	-	-	-	-
Other rodent	-	60	-	-	-	-	-	-
Rabbit	-	732	625	-	-	-	-	-
Cat	-	-	-	-	-	-	-	-
Dog								
Beagle	-	52	3	-	-	36	-	-
Greyhound	-	-	-	-	-	-	-	-
Other including cross-bred dogs	-	-	-	-	-	-	-	-
Ferret	-	-	-	-	-	-	-	-
Other carnivore	-	-	-	-	-	-	-	-
equids	-	-	-	-	-	-	-	-
Pig	-	-	-	-	-	-	-	-
Goat	-	16	-	-	-	-	-	-
Sheep	-	-	-	-	-	-	-	-
Cattle	-	9	-	-	-	-	-	-
Deer	-	-	-	-	-	-	-	-
Camelid	-	-	-	-	-	-	-	-
Other ungulate	-	-	-	-	-	-	-	-

(2) Following a Government decision in 1998, procedures using animals in research on finished cosmetics and on cosmetic ingredients have not been allowed.

Table 9 Scientific procedures (toxicology) by species of animal and toxicological purpose, page 2 of 4

Great Britain 2012								Number of procedures
Species of animal	Toxicology or other safety/efficacy evaluation							
	General safety/efficacy evaluation							
	Pollution	Agriculture	Industry	Household	Food additives	Other foodstuffs	Finished cosmetics(2)	Cosmetics ingredients(2)
Primate								
Prosimian	-	-	-	-	-	-	-	-
New World monkey								
marmoset, tamarin	-	-	-	-	-	-	-	-
Squirrel, owl, spider monkey	-	-	-	-	-	-	-	-
Other New World monkey	-	-	-	-	-	-	-	-
Old World monkey								
Macaque	-	-	-	-	-	-	-	-
Baboon	-	-	-	-	-	-	-	-
Other Old World monkey	-	-	-	-	-	-	-	-
Ape								
Gibbon	-	-	-	-	-	-	-	-
Great Ape	-	-	-	-	-	-	-	-
Other mammal								
Bird								
Domestic fowl (Gallus domesticus)	-	157	-	-	120	-	-	-
Turkey	-	-	-	-	-	-	-	-
Quail (Coturnix coturnix)	-	-	-	-	-	-	-	-
Quail (not Coturnix coturnix)	-	550	-	-	-	-	-	-
Other bird	-	1,231	-	-	-	-	-	-
Reptile - any reptilian species	-	-	-	-	-	-	-	-
Amphibian - any amphibian species	400	-	-	-	-	-	-	-
Fish - any fish species	8,150	2,989	796	-	-	-	-	-
Total	**8,550**	**20,699**	**44,787**	**-**	**669**	**332**	**-**	**-**
Increase on 2011	-5,126	-2,086	25,584	0	-2,855	-3,757	0	0
Percentage change from 2011	-37%	-9%	133%	N/A	-81%	-92%	N/A	N/A
Percentage of total for 2012	2%	5%	12%	0.0%	0.2%	0.1%	0.0%	0.0%
2011 Totals	13,676	22,785	19,203	0	3,524	4,089	0	0

N/A = Not applicable

(2) Following a Government decision in 1998, procedures using animals in research on finished cosmetics and on cosmetic ingredients have not been allowed.

Table 9 Scientific procedures (toxicology) by species of animal and toxicological purpose, page 3 of 4

Great Britain 2012

Number of procedures

Species of animal	Toxicology or other safety/efficacy evaluation								Other	Total
	Pharmaceutical safety/efficacy evaluation			ADME and residue	Toxicology research	Tobacco safety(1)	Other purposes			
	Safety testing	Efficacy testing	Quality control				Medical device safety	Method development		
Mammal										
Mouse	31,525	6,299	117,240	9,905	561	-	1,080	4,863	1,147	184,044
Rat	47,514	148	1,228	9,218	393	-	-	3,835	1,504	111,527
Guinea pig	4,813	-	3,379	-	-	-	-	60	-	8,252
Hamster	900	-	12	72	-	-	-	-	-	984
Gerbil	-	-	-	-	-	-	-	-	-	-
Other rodent	-	-	-	-	-	-	-	-	110	170
Rabbit	5,218	9	3,017	24	-	-	175	144	44	9,988
Cat	-	-	-	-	-	-	-	-	-	-
Dog										
Beagle	2,687	42	4	735	-	-	-	238	1	3,798
Greyhound	-	-	-	-	-	-	-	-	-	-
Other including cross-bred dogs	-	-	-	-	-	-	-	-	-	-
Ferret	-	-	-	-	-	-	-	-	-	-
Other carnivore	16	22	-	-	-	-	-	-	-	38
Horse and other equids	-	100	-	6	-	-	-	-	-	106
Pig	980	816	-	87	11	-	-	41	-	1,935
Goat	-	-	-	-	-	-	-	-	-	16
Sheep	145	105	135	27	-	-	27	-	-	439
Cattle	43	414	10	104	-	-	-	11	-	591
Deer	-	-	-	-	-	-	-	-	-	-
Camelid	-	-	-	-	-	-	-	-	-	-
Other ungulate	-	-	-	-	-	-	-	-	-	-

(1) Following a Government decision in 1997, procedures using animals in research on tobacco have not been allowed.

Table 9 Scientific procedures (toxicology) by species of animal and toxicological purpose, page 4 of 4

Great Britain 2012   Number of procedures

Species of animal	Toxicology or other safety/efficacy evaluation									Total
	Pharmaceutical safety/efficacy evaluation					Other purposes				
	Safety testing	Efficacy testing	Quality control	ADME and residue	Toxicology research	Tobacco safety(1)	Medical device safety	Method development	Other	
Primate										
Prosimian	-	-	-	-	-	-	-	-	-	-
New World monkey										
marmoset, tamarin	10	19	-	13	-	-	-	-	-	**42**
Squirrel, owl, spider monkey	-	-	-	-	-	-	-	-	-	-
Other New World monkey	-	-	-	-	-	-	-	-	-	-
Old World monkey										
Macaque	1,712	5	-	334	-	-	-	217	-	**2,268**
Baboon	-	-	-	-	-	-	-	-	-	-
Other Old World monkey	-	-	-	-	-	-	-	-	-	-
Ape										
Gibbon	-	-	-	-	-	-	-	-	-	-
Great Ape	-	-	-	-	-	-	-	-	-	-
Other mammal	-	-	-	-	-	-	-	-	-	-
Bird										
Domestic fowl (Gallus domesticus)	1,790	11,511	880	54	-	-	-	108	394	**15,014**
Turkey	710	232	-	-	-	-	-	-	-	**942**
Quail (Coturnix coturnix)	-	-	-	-	-	-	-	-	-	-
Quail (not Coturnix coturnix)	-	-	-	-	-	-	-	-	-	**550**
Other bird	-	-	-	-	-	-	-	-	-	**1,231**
Reptile - any reptilian species	-	-	-	-	-	-	-	-	-	-
Amphibian - any amphibian species	-	-	-	-	-	-	-	-	4	**404**
Fish - any fish species	10,227	6,191	-	1,039	-	-	-	5,318	-	**34,710**
Total	**108,290**	**25,913**	**125,905**	**21,618**	**965**	**-**	**1,282**	**14,835**	**3,204**	**377,049**
Increase on 2011	-46,604	2,560	15,619	118	-1,180	0	-957	-2,670	-723	-22,077
Percentage change from 2011	-30%	11%	14%	1%	-55%	N/A	-43%	-15%	-18%	-6%
Percentage of total for 2012	29%	7%	33%	6%	0.3%	0.0%	0.3%	4%	1%	100%
Total	154,894	23,353	110,286	21,500	2,145	0	2,239	17,505	3,927	399,126

(1) Following a Government decision in 1997, procedures using animals in research on tobacco have not been allowed.

N/A = Not applicable

45

Table 9a Animals used (toxicology), by species of animal and toxicological purpose, page 1 of 4

Great Britain 2012

| Species of animal | Toxicology or other safety/efficacy evaluation | | | | | | | |
| | | | General safety/efficacy evaluation | | | | | |
	Pollution	Agriculture	Industry	Household	Food additives	Other foodstuffs	Finished cosmetics(2)	Cosmetics ingredients (2)
Mammal								
Mouse	-	4,275	6,993	-	114	42	-	-
Rat	-	10,628	36,370	-	435	254	-	-
Guinea pig	-	-	-	-	-	-	-	-
Hamster	-	-	-	-	-	-	-	-
Gerbil	-	-	-	-	-	-	-	-
Other rodent	-	60	-	-	-	-	-	-
Rabbit	-	732	625	-	-	-	-	-
Cat	-	-	-	-	-	-	-	-
Dog								
Beagle	-	49	3	-	-	36	-	-
Greyhound	-	-	-	-	-	-	-	-
Other including cross-bred dogs	-	-	-	-	-	-	-	-
Ferret	-	-	-	-	-	-	-	-
Other carnivore	-	-	-	-	-	-	-	-
Horse and other equids	-	-	-	-	-	-	-	-
Pig	-	-	-	-	-	-	-	-
Goat	-	16	-	-	-	-	-	-
Sheep	-	-	-	-	-	-	-	-
Cattle	-	9	-	-	-	-	-	-
Deer	-	-	-	-	-	-	-	-
Camelid	-	-	-	-	-	-	-	-
Other ungulate	-	-	-	-	-	-	-	-

(2)Following a Government decision in 1998, procedures using animals in research on finished cosmetics and on cosmetic ingredients have not been allowed.

Table 9a Animals used (toxicology), by species of animal and toxicological purpose, page 2 of 4

Great Britain 2012 · Number of animals

Species of animal	Toxicology or other safety/efficacy evaluation							
			General safety/efficacy evaluation					
	Pollution	Agriculture	Industry	Household	Food additives	Other foodstuffs	Finished cosmetics(2)	Cosmetics ingredients (2)
Primate								
Prosimian	-	-	-	-	-	-	-	-
New World monkey								
marmoset, tamarin	-	-	-	-	-	-	-	-
Squirrel, owl, spider monkey	-	-	-	-	-	-	-	-
Other New World monkey	-	-	-	-	-	-	-	-
Old World monkey								
Macaque	-	-	-	-	-	-	-	-
Baboon	-	-	-	-	-	-	-	-
Other Old World monkey	-	-	-	-	-	-	-	-
Ape								
Gibbon	-	-	-	-	-	-	-	-
Great Ape	-	-	-	-	-	-	-	-
Other mammal	-	-	-	-	-	-	-	-
Bird								
Domestic fowl (*Gallus domesticus*)	-	114	-	-	120	-	-	-
Turkey	-	-	-	-	-	-	-	-
Quail (*Coturnix coturnix*)	-	-	-	-	-	-	-	-
Quail (not *Coturnix coturnix*)	-	550	-	-	-	-	-	-
Other bird	-	1,231	-	-	-	-	-	-
Reptile - any reptilian species	-	-	-	-	-	-	-	-
Amphibian - any amphibian species	400	-	-	-	-	-	-	-
Fish - any fish species	8,150	2,989	796	-	-	-	-	-
Cephalopod - *Octopus vulgaris*	-	-	-	-	-	-	-	-
Total	**8,550**	**20,653**	**44,787**	**-**	**669**	**332**	**-**	**-**

(2)Following a Government decision in 1998, procedures using animals in research on finished cosmetics and on cosmetic ingredients have not been allowed.

Table 9a Animals used (toxicology), by species of animal and toxicological purpose, page 3 of 4

Great Britain 2012

Number of animals

| Species of animal | Toxicology or other safety/efficacy evaluation | | | | | | | | | Total |
| | Pharmaceutical safety/efficacy evaluation | | | | | Other purposes | | | | |
	Safety testing	Efficacy testing	Quality control	ADME and residue	Toxicology research	Tobacco safety (1)	Medical device safety	Method development	Other	
Mammal										
Mouse	31,525	6,299	117,240	9,905	561	-	1,080	4,659	1,147	183,840
Rat	47,307	148	1,222	9,215	393	-	-	2,975	1,490	110,437
Guinea pig	4,813	-	3,379	-	-	-	-	60	-	8,252
Hamster	900	-	12	72	-	-	-	-	-	984
Gerbil	-	-	-	-	-	-	-	-	-	-
Other rodent	-	-	-	-	-	-	-	-	110	170
Rabbit	3,518	9	1,729	23	-	-	175	34	44	6,889
Cat	-	-	-	-	-	-	-	-	-	-
Dog										
Beagle	2,435	42	4	182	-	-	-	61	-	2,812
Greyhound	-	-	-	-	-	-	-	-	-	-
Other including cross-bred dogs	-	-	-	-	-	-	-	-	-	-
Ferret	-	-	-	-	-	-	-	-	-	-
Other carnivore	12	15	-	-	-	-	-	-	-	27
Horse and other equids	-	87	-	6	-	-	-	-	-	93
Pig	952	800	-	51	11	-	-	31	-	1,845
Goat	-	-	-	-	-	-	-	-	-	16
Sheep	135	105	133	27	-	-	27	-	-	427
Cattle	43	381	10	104	-	-	-	11	-	558
Deer	-	-	-	-	-	-	-	-	-	-
Camelid	-	-	-	-	-	-	-	-	-	-
Other ungulate	-	-	-	-	-	-	-	-	-	-

(1)Following a Government decision in 1997, procedures using animals in research on tobacco have not been allowed.

Table 9a Animals used (toxicology), by species of animal and toxicological purpose, page 4 of 4

Great Britain 2012

Number of animals

| Species of animal | Toxicology or other safety/efficacy evaluation | | | | | | | | | Total |
| | Pharmaceutical safety/efficacy evaluation | | | | | Other purposes | | | | |
	Safety testing	Efficacy testing	Quality control	ADME and residue	Toxicology research	Tobacco safety (1)	Medical device safety	Method development	Other	
Primate										
Prosimian	-	-	-	-	-	-	-	-	-	-
New World monkey										
marmoset, tamarin	-	-	-	7	-	-	-	-	-	7
Squirrel, owl, spider monkey	-	-	-	-	-	-	-	-	-	-
Other New World monkey	-	-	-	-	-	-	-	-	-	-
Old World monkey										
Macaque	1,539	3	-	105	-	-	-	130	-	1,777
Baboon	-	-	-	-	-	-	-	-	-	-
Other Old World monkey	-	-	-	-	-	-	-	-	-	-
Ape										
Gibbon	-	-	-	-	-	-	-	-	-	-
Great Ape	-	-	-	-	-	-	-	-	-	-
Other mammal	-	-	-	-	-	-	-	-	-	-
Bird										
Domestic fowl (Gallus domesticus)	1,790	11,511	880	54	-	-	-	108	394	14,971
Turkey	710	232	-	-	-	-	-	-	-	942
Quail (Coturnix coturnix)	-	-	-	-	-	-	-	-	-	-
Quail (not Coturnix coturnix)	-	-	550	-	-	-	-	-	-	550
Other bird	-	-	-	-	-	-	-	-	-	1,231
Reptile - any reptilian species	-	-	-	-	-	-	-	-	-	-
Amphibian - any amphibian species	-	-	-	-	-	-	-	-	4	404
Fish - any fish species	10,227	6,191	-	1,039	-	-	-	5,318	-	34,710
Cephalopod - Octopus vulgaris	-	-	-	-	-	-	-	-	-	-
Total	105,906	25,823	124,609	20,790	965	-	1,282	13,387	3,189	370,942

(1)Following a Government decision in 1997, procedures using animals in research on tobacco have not been allowed.

Table 10 Scientific procedures (toxicology) by species of animal and type of legislation

Summary version

Note. For numbers of procedures by purpose, see full table available on the website

Great Britain 2012

Species of animal	UK requirements only	One EU country only (not UK)	EU requirements, incl. European Pharmacopoeia	Requirements of (non-EU) Council of Europe	Requirements of other countries	Any combination of legislative requirements	Non-legislative purposes	Number of procedures Total
Mammal								
Mouse	411	-	6,243	-	9,796	163,220	4,374	**184,044**
Rat	169	-	5,661	-	110	101,072	4,515	**111,527**
All other rodents	67	-	955	-	342	8,042	-	**9,406**
Rabbit	112	-	3,197	-	48	6,314	317	**9,988**
Cat	-	-	-	-	-	-	-	**-**
Dog	-	-	42	-	-	3,617	139	**3,798**
Ferret	-	-	-	-	-	-	-	**-**
Other carnivore	38	-	-	-	-	-	-	**38**
Horse and other equids	-	-	41	-	-	65	-	**106**
Pigs, sheep & all other ungulates	-	-	1,141	-	3	1,745	92	**2,981**
Primate								
New World monkey	-	-	-	-	-	42	-	**42**
Old World monkey	-	-	-	-	-	2,200	68	**2,268**
All other mammals	-	-	-	-	-	-	-	**-**
Bird	-	-	2,366	-	1,005	14,162	204	**17,737**
Reptile / Amphibian	-	-	-	-	-	404	-	**404**
Fish	1,386	-	5,403	-	534	13,230	14,157	**34,710**
Total	**2,183**	**-**	**25,049**	**-**	**11,838**	**314,113**	**23,866**	**377,049**
Increase on 2011	-1,088	-1,562	-2,353	-46	9,298	15,492	-41,818	-22,077
Percentage change from 2011	-33%	-100%	-9%	N/A	366%	5%	-64%	-6%
Percentage of total for 2012	1%	0.0%	7%	0.0%	3%	83%	6%	100%
2011 Totals	3,271	1,562	27,402	46	2,540	298,621	65,684	399,126

N/A = Not applicable

50

Great Britain 2012

Number of procedures

Table 11 Scientific procedures (toxicology) by species of animal and type of toxicological test: all purposes, page 1 of 2

Species of animal	Type of toxicological test or procedure									
	Acute lethal toxicity	Acute lethal concentration	Acute limit setting	Acute non-lethal clinical sign	Subacute limit-setting or dose ranging	Subacute toxicity	Subchronic and chronic	Carcinogenicity	Genetic toxicology (includes mutagenicity)	Teratogenicity
Mammal										
Mouse	97,236	845	1,344	10,709	2,010	2,104	2,467	2,803	2,323	294
Rat	57	1,404	2,576	4,440	8,233	13,392	6,897	5,154	3,311	2,700
All other rodents	-	110	-	40	-	-	-	650	-	-
Rabbit	10	-	-	30	61	146	60	-	-	1,344
Cat	-	-	-	-	-	-	-	-	-	-
Dog	-	-	-	38	458	1,399	420	-	-	-
Ferret	-	-	-	-	-	-	-	-	-	-
Other carnivore	-	-	-	-	-	-	-	-	-	-
Horse and other equids	-	-	-	-	-	-	-	-	-	-
Pigs, sheep & all other ungulates	-	-	-	-	50	133	118	-	-	-
Primate										
New World monkey	-	-	-	-	10	-	-	-	-	-
Old World monkey	-	-	-	-	271	690	728	-	-	-
All other mammals	-	-	-	-	-	-	-	-	-	-
Bird	660	330	269	-	66	1,132	-	-	-	-
Reptile, amphibian	-	-	-	-	-	400	-	-	-	-
Fish	-	5,362	2,908	-	360	5,038	3,320	-	-	-
Total	**97,963**	**8,051**	**7,097**	**15,257**	**11,529**	**24,434**	**14,010**	**8,607**	**5,634**	**4,338**
Increase on 2011	18,593	-632	-3,378	-1,862	-2,814	-1,788	-4,224	4,760	-1,382	-817
Percentage change from 2011	23%	-7%	-32%	-11%	-20%	-7%	-23%	124%	-20%	-16%
Percentage of total for 2012	26%	2%	2%	4%	3%	6%	4%	2%	1%	1%
2011 Totals	79,370	8,683	10,475	17,119	14,343	26,222	18,234	3,847	7,016	5,155

51

Table 11 Scientific procedures (toxicology) by species of animal and type of toxicological test: all purposes, page 2 of 2

Great Britain 2012

| Species of animal | Type of toxicological test or procedure | | | | | | | | | | Number of procedures |
	Other reproductive toxicity	In eyes	For skin Irritation	For skin sensitisation	Toxicokinetics	Pyrogenicity	Biocompatibility	Enzyme induction for in vitro tests	Immunotoxicology	Other toxicology	Total
Mammal											
Mouse	1,092	-	115	982	6,689	-	700	-	7,641	44,690	184,044
Rat	40,044	-	-	-	8,072	-	-	148	290	14,809	111,527
All other rodents	-	-	-	-	72	-	-	-	-	8,534	9,406
Rabbit	156	712	595	-	8	4,655	236	-	-	1,975	9,988
Cat	82	-	-	-	-	-	-	-	-	1,123	-
Dog	82	-	-	-	278	-	-	-	-	1,123	3,798
Ferret	-	-	-	-	-	-	-	-	-	-	-
Other carnivore	-	-	-	-	-	-	-	-	-	38	38
Horse and other equids	-	-	-	-	6	-	-	-	-	100	106
Pigs, sheep & all other ungulates	-	-	-	-	125	-	63	-	-	2,482	2,981
Primate											
New World monkey	-	-	-	-	6	-	-	-	-	26	42
Old World monkey	-	-	-	-	202	-	-	-	-	377	2,268
All other mammals	-	-	-	-	-	-	-	-	-	-	-
Bird	456	-	-	-	127	-	-	-	-	14,697	17,737
Reptile, amphibian	-	-	-	-	-	-	-	-	-	4	404
Fish	885	-	-	-	378	-	-	-	-	16,459	34,710
Total	42,715	712	710	982	15,963	4,655	999	148	7,931	105,314	377,049
Increase on 2011	6,236	20	-391	-372	-3,873	374	358	-114	-5,196	-25,575	-22,077
Percentage change from 2011	17%	3%	-36%	-27%	-20%	9%	56%	-44%	-40%	-19.5%	-6%
Percentage of total for 2012	11%	0.2%	0.2%	0.3%	4%	1%	0.3%	0.0%	2%	28%	100%
2011 Totals	36,479	692	1,101	1,354	19,836	4,281	641	262	13,127	130,889	399,126

Appendix A

General system of control under the Animals (Scientific Procedures) Act 1986.

Introduction

1. The Animals (Scientific Procedures) Act 1986 puts into effect a rigorous system of controls on scientific work on living animals, including the need for: both the researcher and the project to be separately licensed; stringent safeguards on animal pain and suffering; and general requirements to ensure the care and welfare of animals. The Act implements, and in some ways exceeds, the requirements of European Union Directive 86/609/EEC.

2. Operation of the Act is a reserved issue in Great Britain, the Home Office administering the legislation in England, Scotland and Wales. The Act is separately administered in Northern Ireland.

Scope of the Act

3. The 1986 Act controls any experimental or other scientific procedure applied to a 'protected animal' which may have the effect of causing that animal pain, suffering, distress or lasting harm. Such work is referred to in the Act as a 'regulated procedure'.

4. 'Protected animals' are defined as all living vertebrate animals, except man, plus one invertebrate species, Octopus vulgaris. The definition extends to fetal, larval or embryonic forms that have reached specified stages in their development.

5. Under the Act an animal is regarded as 'living' until "the permanent cessation of circulation or complete destruction of its brain". Procedures carried out on decerebrate animals are also subject to the controls of the Act.

6. The definition of a regulated procedure encompasses most breeding of animals with genetic defects; production of antisera and other blood products; the maintenance and passage of tumours and parasites; and the administration for a scientific purpose of an anaesthetic, analgesic, tranquilliser or other drug to dull perception. Killing an animal requires licence authority in certain circumstances.

7. The controls of the 1986 Act do not extend to procedures applied to animals in the course of recognised veterinary, agricultural or animal husbandry practice; procedures for the identification of animals for scientific purposes, if this causes no more than momentary pain or distress and no lasting harm; or the administration of a novel veterinary product under authority of an Animal Test Exemption Certificate (issued under the Medicines Act 1968).

8. Two kinds of licence are required for all work controlled by the Act. The procedures must be part of a programme of work authorised by a project licence and the person applying the regulated procedures must hold a personal licence. No work may be done unless the procedure, the animals used and the place where the work is to be done are specifically authorised in both project and personal licences.

Personal licences

9. A personal licence is the Home Secretary's endorsement that the holder is a suitable and competent person to carry out specified procedures on specified animals, under

supervision where necessary. Applicants must be over 18 and are required to give details of their qualifications, training and experience. Those who have not previously held a Home Office licence need the endorsement of a sponsor (usually a personal licence holder in a senior position at the applicant's place of work). Satisfactory completion of an accredited training course is also required before a personal licence is issued.

10.   On 31 December 2012 there were 14,875 active personal licences. Personal licences continue to be in force until revoked but they must be reviewed at least every five years.

Project licences

11.   A project licence is granted when the Home Secretary considers that the use of living animals in a programme of work, for a purpose permitted by the Act, is justified and the methods proposed appropriate.

12.   In deciding whether and on what terms to authorise the project, the likely adverse effects on the animals used must be weighed against the potential benefits (to humans, other animals or the environment) which are expected to accrue from the work. Adequate consideration must also have been given to the feasibility of using alternative methods not involving living animals.

13.   The holder of a project licence undertakes overall responsibility for the scientific direction and control of the work. New project licence applicants are required to complete an accredited training course before the licence is granted.

14.   When making an application for a project licence the applicant nominates, and the Home Office assigns, an overall severity banding to the project. There are three main severity bandings: mild, moderate and substantial. A fourth band, unclassified, is used for procedures where the animals are decerebrate or used under terminal anaesthesia – i.e. the animal is anaesthetised before the procedure starts, is kept anaesthetised throughout the course of the procedure and is killed without recovering consciousness.

15.   The severity band depends not only upon the amount of suffering caused but also the duration, the number of animals and what action is taken to reduce suffering, such as the use of anaesthesia or early end-points. The overall severity is used in weighing the likely adverse effects on the animals against the benefits likely to accrue, as required by section 5(4) of the Act.

16.   The following table details the number of project licences which were active on 31 December 2012, the number granted during 2012 and the number revoked during 2012 (usually either at the licence holder's request or because the licence had run the maximum allowed term of five years). The total figures are subdivided into severity bandings.

Project licences by severity band – number and share of total, 2012

Severity band	In force on 31 December 2012		Granted during 2012		Revoked during 2012	
	Number	%	Number	%	Number	%
Mild	969	36%	239	38%	197	38%
Moderate	1647	61%	366	58%	306	59%
Substantial	56	2%	9	1%	9	2%
Unclassified	45	2%	13	2%	10	2%
Total	2717		627		522	

NB Percentages may not sum to 100 due to rounding.

Designation of premises

17. Except where otherwise authorised in a project licence (e.g. for field work at a specified place and time), any place where work is carried out under the Act must be designated as a scientific procedure establishment. Since January 1990 establishments that breed certain types of animal listed in Schedule 2 of the Act – mice, rats, guinea pigs, hamsters, rabbits, dogs, cats and primates – for use in scientific procedures ('breeding establishments'), and establishments that obtain such animals from elsewhere and supply them to laboratories ('supplying establishments') must hold a certificate of designation.

18. Quail (Coturnix coturnix) was added to the list of species specified in Schedule 2 of the Act in 1993, and ferrets, gerbils, genetically modified pigs and genetically modified sheep were added to the list in 1999. Designated establishments are required to nominate a person to be responsible for the day-to-day care of animals and a veterinary surgeon to advise on their health and welfare.

19. There were 176 certificates of designation in force on 31 December 2012. Of these, 175 were registered as user establishments, 114 as breeding establishments and 65 as supplying establishments. These figures add up to more than the total number of establishments because a single establishment may fall into more than one of the categories: for example, an establishment may be registered as both a breeder and user of animals.

Table 19 Project licences and scientific procedures by type of designated establishment

Great Britain 2012

Type of designated establishment	Number of licence holders[1] reporting countable[2] procedures, by number of procedures reported									Licensees reporting non-countable[2] procedures only	Number of licence holders[1] reporting no procedures	Total licensees	Procedures	
	Number of procedures reported												Total	Percentage
	1 to 50	51 to 100	101 to 200	201 to 400	401 to 600	601 to 800	801 to 1,000	More than 1,000	Total					
Public health laboratories	11	1	1	2	3	-	-	4	22	2	4	28	14,167	0%
Universities, medical schools	383	208	240	295	157	109	91	451	1,934	9	524	2,467	1,967,030	48%
NHS hospitals	2	3	4	5	2	1	-	6	23	-	5	28	21,882	1%
Government departments	28	7	8	9	3	1	4	12	72	-	26	98	79,598	2%
Other public bodies	28	11	12	17	9	12	3	75	167	2	57	226	549,463	13%
Non-profit-making organisations	19	11	8	8	8	3	4	47	108	-	18	126	352,043	9%
Commercial organisations	36	12	17	25	20	11	8	88	217	2	47	266	1,125,845	27%
Total	507	253	290	361	202	137	110	683	2,543	15	681	3,239	4,110,028	100%

(1) Some licence-holders hold more than one licence; these figures are compiled **by numbers of project licences,** not by numbers of actual licence-holders.

(2) Only procedures on adult or free-living animals (including neonatal and juvenile mammals, and newly-hatched birds) are counted.
Details of procedures on immature forms (e.g. larvae, embryos) are collected but not counted.
Animals in the wild involved in rodenticide trials are also not counted. Details (if applicable) are given in the Commentary.